Theater

VOLUME 51, NUMBER 1

T0327030

TOM SELLAR, *Editor*

YALE SCHOOL OF DRAMA
YALE REPERTORY THEATRE

EDITOR Tom Sellar

ASSOCIATE EDITOR Madeline Charne

MANAGING EDITORS Lily Haje and Nicholas Orvis

MANAGING EDITOR, WEB PROJECTS Ashley M. Thomas

ADVISORY BOARD James Bundy, Victoria Nolan, Catherine Sheehy

CONTRIBUTING EDITORS Una Chaudhuri, Thomas F. DeFrantz, Liz Diamond, Miriam Felton-Dansky, Elinor Fuchs, Jacob Gallagher-Ross, Gitta Honegger, Shannon Jackson, Jonathan Kalb, Renate Klett, Jennifer Krasinski, James Leverett, Mark Lord, Charles McNulty, Tavia Nyong'o, Ken Reynolds, Joseph Roach, Marc Robinson, Chantal Rodriguez, Gordon Rogoff, Daniel Sack, Alisa Solomon, Andrea Tompa, Paul Walsh

AFFILIATED ARTISTS Marc Bamuthi Joseph, Annie Dorsen, Branden Jacobs-Jenkins, Morgan Jenness, Melanie Joseph, Aaron Landsman, David Levine

Theater is published three times a year (February, May, and November) by Duke University Press, 905 W. Main St., Suite 18B, Durham, NC 27701, on behalf of Yale School of Drama/Yale Repertory Theatre. For a list of the sources in which *Theater* is indexed and abstracted, see dukeupress.edu/theater.

SUBMISSIONS AND
EDITORIAL CORRESPONDENCE
See the Duke University Press *Theater* website for detailed submission guidelines: read.dukeupress.edu/theater. Send manuscripts for submission and letters concerning editorial matters to *Theater*, PO BOX 208244, New Haven, CT 06520-8244; theater.magazine @yale.edu.

PERMISSIONS
Photocopies for course or research use that are supplied to the end user at no cost may be made without explicit permission or fee. Photocopies that are provided to the end user for a fee may not be made without payment of permission fees to Duke University Press. Address requests for permission to republish copyrighted material to Rights and Permissions Manager, permissions @dukeupress.edu.

WORLD WIDE WEB
Visit the journal's website at theatermagazine.org and Duke University Press Journals at dukeupress.edu/journals.

SUBSCRIPTIONS
Direct all orders to Duke University Press, Journals Customer Relations, 905 W. Main St., Suite 18B, Durham, NC 27701. Annual subscription rates: print-plus-electronic institutions, $270; print-only institutions, $257; e-only institutions, $204; e-only individuals, $15; individuals, $30; students, $20. For information on subscriptions to the e-Duke Journals Scholarly Collections, contact libraryrelations@dukeupress.edu. Print subscriptions: add $11 postage and applicable HST (including 5% GST) for Canada; add $14 postage outside the US and Canada. Back volumes (institutions): $257. Single issues: institutions, $86; individuals, $12. For more information, contact Duke University Press Journals at 888-651-0122 (toll-free in the US and Canada) or at 919-688-5134; subscriptions @dukeupress.edu.

ADVERTISEMENTS
Direct inquiries about advertising to Journals Advertising Coordinator, journals_advertising@dukeupress.edu.

© 2021 by Yale School of Drama/ Yale Repertory Theatre
ISSN 0161-0775

CONTRIBUTORS

BASEL ABBAS and RUANNE ABOU-RAHME work together across a range of sound, image, text, installation, and performance artworks. Their practice engages the intersections among performativity, political imaginaries, the body, and virtuality.

MIRNA BAMIEH is an artist and chef whose artworks unpack social concerns and limitations in contemporary political dilemmas and reflect on the conditions that characterize Palestinian communities. In 2017 she founded Palestine Hosting Society as an extension of her art practice to look at the politics of disappearance and memory production.

ALI CHAHROUR is a choreographer and dancer. His research is based on the local quality of movement in contemporary dance, whose techniques and problematics are inspired by its surroundings and history. His work examines relationships among the body, religion, and the sacred, relying on Islamic and Shiite religious rituals and practice.

JASON DE LEÓN is head curator of *Hostile Terrain 94* and executive director of the nonprofit Undocumented Migration Project, Inc. He is also professor of anthropology and Chicana/o studies at the University of California, Los Angeles, and author of the award-winning book *The Land of Open Graves: Living and Dying on the Migrant Trail* (2015). De León is a 2017 MacArthur Foundation Fellow, and between 2013 and 2017 he cocurated the traveling exhibition *State of Exception*.

TANIA EL KHOURY is a live artist creating installations and performances focusing on audience interactivity and its politics. She is a Distinguished Artist in Residence and codirector of the MA in Human Rights and the Arts at Bard College, a 2019 Soros Art Fellow, and the recipient of a Bessie Award and the International Prize for Live Art. Tania holds a PhD in performance studies from Royal Holloway, University of London, and is a cofounder of Dictaphone Group.

RUDI GOBLEN is a writer, dancer, actor, and music producer. He is a member of Teo Castellanos/D-Projects and a recipient of the Future Aesthetics Artist Re-grant, Miami-Dade County's Choreographers Award, and a FEAST Grant for his book *A Bag of Halos and Horns* (2017). He has released five instrumental albums and is currently attending Yale School of Drama for playwriting.

GIDEON LESTER is artistic director of the Fisher Center at Bard and senior curator of the OSUN Center for Human Rights and the Arts. A Tony Award–winning curator, dramaturg, and creative producer, he was cocurator of the Crossing the Line Festival and acting artistic director of the American Repertory Theater.

The PALESTINE HOSTING SOCIETY is a live art project created by Mirna Bamieh that explores traditional food culture in Palestine, especially those that are on the verge of disappearing. The project brings these dishes back to life over dinner tables, talks, walks, and various interventions.

ALEXANDRA RIPP is director of Five College Dance, a collaboration of the dance departments and programs of Mount Holyoke, Smith, Amherst, and Hampshire Colleges and the University of Massachusetts Amherst. She is also a researcher and translator of contemporary Chilean theater and holds a DFA in dramaturgy from Yale School of Drama.

EMILIO ROJAS is a multidisciplinary artist working primarily with the body in performance. He holds an MFA in performance from the School of the Art Institute of Chicago. Rojas utilizes his body in a political and critical way, as an instrument to unearth removed traumas, embodied forms of decolonization, migration, and poetics of space. Besides his artistic practice, he is also an educator, translator, community activist, yoga teacher, and antioppression facilitator with queer, migrant, and refugee youth.

TOM SELLAR is editor of *Theater* and professor in the practice of dramaturgy and dramatic criticism at Yale School of Drama.

ASHLEY M. THOMAS was born and raised in Harlem, New York. She is interested in exploring the intersections of culture, politics, and Beyoncé through a Black feminist lens. She is a second-year MFA candidate in dramaturgy and dramatic criticism at Yale School of Drama.

The UNDOCUMENTED MIGRATION PROJECT, INC., is a long-term anthropological study of clandestine movement between Latin America and the United States that uses ethnography, archaeology, visual anthropology, and forensic science to understand this violent social process and raise awareness through research, education, and public outreach.

CONTENTS

Title Page:
Tania El Khoury's
Cultural Exchange Rate,
LAB Biennial *Where
No Wall Remains*, The
Fisher Center at Bard,
Annandale-on-Hudson,
NY, 2019. Photo: Maria
Baranova

Inside Back Cover:
Ali Chahrour's *Night*,
LAB Biennial *Where
No Wall Remains*, The
Fisher Center at Bard,
Annandale-on-Hudson,
NY, 2019. Photo: Maria
Baranova

The US-Mexico
border fence at
Imperial Beach,
San Diego, 2018.
Photo: Tony
Webster, CC BY

Up Front

Windows and Walls

Tom Sellar

"Where No Wall Remains," the title of this issue, corresponds to a 2019 biennial of live performances and interactive art at Bard College and comes from a love poem by the thirteenth-century Persian poet Rumi. In "The Thief of Sleep" he wrote, "They say there is a window from one heart to another. / How can there be a window where no wall remains?" The festival, which took place in New York's Hudson Valley on the thirtieth anniversary of the fall of the Berlin Wall, commissioned artists, many from the Middle East or Central America, to explore the nature of present-day borders while simultaneously imagining a borderless future. Collected here are the resulting performance texts, dialogues, exhibition dossiers, and artistic notebooks, introduced by the biennial's cocurator, the Lebanese artist Tania El Khoury.

As Thomas Nail stressed in his 2016 book *Theory of the Border*, three decades after the uptick in economic globalization with its promises of mobility, there are now more, not fewer, borders. The events of 9/11 and the wars that followed vastly expanded systems of surveillance and control to maintain divided zones. "Contemporary social motion is everywhere divided," Nail writes; he refers not only to nationalized (or occupied) territories but also to other kinds of domains—economies, institutions, residential communities, even informational zones.[1] Policed, militarized, and enforced with new technologies, these dividing lines demonstrate power structures and demarcate extreme inequities, protecting disparities of wealth and racialized privilege.

Far from presenting obstacles to a globalized political order to be eventually dismantled—the myth, if not lie, of the neoliberal order—borders are now responsible for preserving its structures. They are bitterly contested sites as well as places where desperate migrants struggle to survive. White nationalists in the United States (and elsewhere) call for walls and patrols to exclude those seeking political asylum and relief from war and hunger, walls that right-wing adherents believe will preserve their cultural and racial supremacy. As anthropologist Jason De León (one of the voices in the Live Arts Bard Biennial) demonstrates in his book *The Land of Open Graves*, the US-Mexico border intentionally uses Arizona's Sonoran Desert as a lethal deterrent, resulting in widespread death and brutality that reshapes the economy and communities on either side.[2]

Borders are places, but they are also, Nail writes, sometimes "processes of circulation" and sites of "in-betweenness."[3] The frontiers and limits they are intended to embody reveal much about our violent nation-states and about our collective humanity. The sheer vastness of this oppressive infrastructure, however, can make it hard for those far away to perceive its workings. The scale and pervasiveness of borders also discourage hopes for a freer world. The artists assembled here help us see it more clearly and dare us to hope for another kind of world.

Note: We regret that it was not possible—for practical reasons—to include Emily Jacir's *Letter to a Friend*, an account of the changes on her street in Bethlehem following occupation, migration, and war. Interested readers should be sure to explore her compelling work, which encompasses many media; please visit www.theatermagazine.org for more about Jacir's work. Special thanks are due to photographer Maria Baranova and to the entire Live Arts Bard team, especially Caleb Hammons, for their tireless assistance with this project.

Notes

1. Thomas Nail, *Theory of the Border* (New York: Oxford University Press, 2016), 1.
2. Jason De León, *The Land of Open Graves: Living and Dying on the Migrant Trail* (Oakland: University of California Press, 2015).
3. Nail, *Theory of the Border*, 1.

Theater 51:1   DOI 10.1215/01610775-8824687
© 2021 by Tom Sellar

Pandemic Performances
The Viral Triumph of Las Tesis

Alexandra Ripp

On June 16, 2020, members of the Chilean feminist performance collective Las Tesis learned that the national police force was suing them for saying four sentences. The Caribineros of Chile alleged that part of group's May video collaboration with Moscow-based arts group Pussy Riot, which included the words *fuego a los pacos* (fire on the police), constituted "a direct and public incitement to act violently against [them]."[1] Although Las Tesis deleted the offending line, the charge stands and has spurred widespread support for the accused. Petitions circulating within Chile and Latin America defend the group's right to artistic expression, while organizations such as PEN America and the Inter-American Committee on Human Rights officially condemned this criminalization of free speech. In late July (a week prior to this writing), several high-profile US artists and activists, plus Pussy Riot member Nadya Tolokonnikova, issued a petition that has almost eight thousand signatures.

Such strong public opposition to and support for Las Tesis signals its central place in both Chilean and international uprisings. Unrest in Chile began in October 2019, when President Sebastián Piñera raised the metro fare by about four US cents—an impossibility for minimum-wage workers. High school students organized a massive nonviolent fare evasion campaign, and the government responded by deploying thousands of troops, declaring a state of emergency, and imposing curfews. Barring the 2010 earthquake, Chile has not been under such restrictions since Augusto Pinochet's 1973–90 dictatorship. Indeed, the state's tanks, tear gas, and water cannons on the streets evoked the traumatic coup that secured Pinochet's power.

The dictatorship's ghosts, which have quietly loomed over Chile for three decades, have returned to full view. The state's brutal response unleashed Chileans' long-simmering anger about structural injustice inherited from the Pinochet regime, which (influenced by the ideas of US economist Milton Friedman and supported by the US government) turned the nation into a testing ground for neoliberalism. The post-dictatorship government did not fully dismantle the resulting privatized system, due to both legal restrictions and a strategic emphasis on building national unity over confronting the divisive past. Consequently, the Caribineros' structure, methods, and personnel have remained relatively unaltered, even though between 1973 and 1990 they had killed over three thousand innocent victims, tortured thirty-eight thousand, and exiled hundreds of thousands more.[2]

Until recently, this destructive legacy has not been highly visible on the international stage. Despite its vaunted reputation for its high per-capita income and investor-friendly environment, Chile has the worst income inequality in the thirty-nation Organisation for Economic Co-operation and Development.[3] While Chileans have protested various issues in the last decade, they now demand total transformation: an

Las Tesis's *Un violador en tu camino*, Women's Day protest, Concepción, Chile, 2020. Photo: Isis Fuentealba Quiñones, CC BY-SA

education, health care, and pension system overhaul; a wage increase; gender parity in government; Piñera's resignation; and a new constitution.[4] State forces, however, adhere to Pinochet-era strategies: by December 19, over 12,700 Chileans had been wounded, and the public prosecutor's office had opened over 2,670 criminal investigations into torture, sexual violence, and firearm injuries, mostly by Caribineros personnel.[5] The United Nations accused the police and armed forces of human rights abuses—including, most perversely, intentionally shooting rubber bullets into protestors' eyes.[6]

In November 2019 Las Tesis orchestrated the mass performance of a choreographed feminist anthem, first in Valparaíso and then in Santiago. Per their mission to translate feminist theory into other languages and modes, "Un violador en tu camino" ("The Rapist Is You") animates feminist anthropologist Rita Segato's ideas through female bodies chanting and moving in time.[7] Far from spontaneous, each element of the street performance holds significance: the women's blindfolds allude to the protestors' blinding while rejecting the male gaze, their green scarves connote Argentina's feminist movement Ni Una Menos, their movements index postures of gender oppression, and their rhythmic chant remixes a Caribinero anthem. Through its frank, accusatory text and its unabashed invasion of public space, the performance indicts not just individual aggressors but the patriarchal state as a whole—in Chile and globally—for facilitating violence against women and promoting their ongoing subjugation. Given this critique's broad applicability, the performance's video has gone viral, inspiring women worldwide to reperform the choreography and spoken text.

In spring 2020 Pussy Riot invited Las Tesis to collaborate on a manifesto against police violence, with a focus on Latin America. In Chile, global pandemic seemed to facilitate deeper state repression: an April vote on a new constitution was conveniently postponed, curfews had been reinstated, and new laws put a chill on the many creative works of resistance offered by artists across media, which often occupied the streets and involved gathering. The groups' YouTube collaboration revives Las Tesis's critique of the patriarchal state gripping Chile and draws in all of Latin America. The text, spoken by Las Tesis and Mexican Pussy Riot member Wendy Moira through balaclavas, urges ongoing resistance and mutual aid in order to survive COVID and state oppression alike.

Vocal public support for Las Tesis has been heartening, but Chilean artists and arts institutions are still suffering. As of this writing, curfews have frozen cultural activity, the national arts budget is in jeopardy, and cultural institutions are on hiatus. Since few theaters receive direct public subsidies, most will not survive the pandemic; those that do will contend with limited capacity and an audience base with reduced spending money. As freelancers without strong union support, out-of-work artists—like many others in Chile and like many vulnerable artists in the US—have no economic safety net. The government did offer a COVID emergency fund but it relied on a competitive neoliberal model, similar to its traditional FONDART program, that has angered artists and arts institutions.

If the United States has shared its problems with Chile, Las Tesis and other Chilean artists responding to the crisis now offer us solutions. Chilean playwright-director Guillermo Calderón wrote to me that, in a violent context in which theater artists could not ascertain their art's literal or aesthetic place, Las Tesis' work provided an answer: "It doesn't need a theater and it actually needs the protest to thrive. It's the right theater for this time."[8] Whatever the suit's outcome, Las Tesis has already won.

NOTES

1. Translation by Boris Van der Spek, "Feminist Group Las Tesis Sued for Inciting Violence against Police," *Chile Today*, June 18, 2020, chiletoday.cl/site/feminist-group-las-tesis-sued-for-inciting-violence-against-police/.

2. Pascale Bonnefoy, "Mounting Evidence of Abuse by Chile's Police Leads to Calls for Reform," *New York Times*, December 13, 2020, www.nytimes.com/2019/12/13/world/americas/chile-police-protests.html.

3. Aislinn Laing, Dave Sherwood, and Fabian Cambero, "Explainer: Chile's Inequality Challenge: What Went Wrong and What Can Be Fixed?," *Reuters*, October 23, 2019, www.reuters.com/article/us-chile-protests-explainer/explainer-chiles-inequality-challenge-what-went-wrong-and-can-it-be-fixed-idUSKBN1X22RK.

4. Jennifer Joan Thompson, "How to Do Things with Theses: Chile's National Police Force Sues the Feminist Artistic Collective, Las Tesis," *CounterPunch*, July 3, 2020, www.counterpunch.org/2020/07/03/how-to-do-things-with-theses-chiles-national-police-force-sues-the-feminist-artistic-collective-las-tesis/.

5. Bonnefoy, "Mounting Evidence of Abuse."

6. "Chile Protests: UN Accuses Security Forces of Human Rights Abuses," CNN, December 13, 2019, www.bbc.com/news/world-latin-america-50779466.

7. Ana María Enciso Noguera, "How Performance Art Has United Women's Voices in Latin America and throughout the World," *Al Día*, December 3, 2019, aldianews.com/articles/culture/how-performance-art-has-united-womens-voices-latin-america-and-throughout-world.

8. Guillermo Calderón, text message to author, July 26, 2020.

Theater 51:1   DOI 10.1215/01610775-8824701

CALL AND (LACK OF) RESPONSE

Ashley M. Thomas

There are two pandemics in our country right now: COVID-19 and racism. Both are claiming the lives of innocent people. The entire nation remains in an inchoate phase of recovery, but the onus for American theaters to address one aspect of the pandemics is increasingly evident. As the country reckons with growing state violence and anti-

The lobby of the Huntington Theatre Company's Stanford Calderwood Pavilion, Boston, as seen in social media posts, 2020. Courtesy of Huntington Theatre Company

Blackness, theater organizations have been called on to address their own institution-alized racism. According to a 2019 *American Theatre* article, among seventy-five LORT theaters, only six have people of color leading them.[1] (This statistic may have changed slightly this year, given subsequent, high-profile appointments at venues such as Long Wharf Theatre and Oregon Shakespeare Festival.) Before the pandemics, racial justice had been coming slowly but surely; with tensions in the country boiling over, there's too much at stake to be precious with time.

For activists, it started in the streets in the immediate aftermath of the mur-der of George Floyd by the Minneapolis police, although Black Lives Matter activists have been active since 2011. For theaters, it started on Twitter. Anonymous artists and organizers created the #OpenYourLobby hashtag and Twitter account in June 2020 to pressure theater organizations to contribute meaningfully to the protests. Theater com-panies, whose doors have otherwise been shuttered during the health crisis, joined in, announcing that they would provide water, snacks, and restroom access for Black Lives Matter protestors. There was a flurry of support from New York–based cultural organi-zations, including the Public Theater, Atlantic Theater Company, and even the Brook-lyn Museum. But the anonymous Twitter account that championed the hashtag has been inactive since July 6. Since this initial expression of good will, theaters have been relatively quiet.

Prior to the #OpenYourLobby campaign, many organizations had remained muted until a publicly accessible Google document titled "Theaters Not Speaking Out" went viral on May 30. Activist Marie Cisco created the spreadsheet to track names of com-panies that had not yet issued a statement against the anti-Blackness experienced particularly through the state violence at the helm of George Floyd's and Breonna Taylor's deaths. Under pressure, statements flurried in, taking over theaters' social media accounts and websites, and in a rare case, in the form of mass emails to patrons. Some explicitly affirmed "Black Lives Matter" while others mentioned more vague messages of solidarity.

But while theaters seemed to finally find their voice, theater makers did too. A callout soon followed from a collective of Black, Indigenous, and People of Color (BIPOC) theater makers who founded the online platform We See You, White American Theater. According to their website, it started off as an initial conversation with three people and then expanded to a Zoom call with thirty, in which the activists discussed how "racism and white supremacy have also corrupted and shaped our theater institutions, ranging from the universities to not-for-profit and commercial houses." That small but mighty group of thirty grew to three hundred. When the statement was finally released, over eighty thousand people signed.[2] In their inaugural letter, artists chronicled the tokenization of BIPOC art, as well as more aggressive forms of racism, such as inequitable hiring processes. The organizers have since released a twenty-nine-page list of demands for reformed or altered professional practices. Demands include affinity spaces in theater organizations and unions, contracted intimacy directors for every production, and ad boycotts for newspapers lacking BIPOC theater critics.[3]

And yet again, many theaters stayed relatively quiet in response.

In an industry where words lead the worlds we imagine, are the earlier messages of solidarity smoke and mirrors or a step toward a more inclusive industry? To some, their attempts seem futile. BIPOC theater activists are expecting the altering of the status quo to go further; theaters need to do far more than just release statements on equity, diversity, and inclusion—it is time to announce plans, act on action items, and begin antiracist trainings. The American theater is not in an impossible position, though. While theaters are fighting for financial stability amid the pandemic, statistics show time and time again that diversity is a sustainable growth model for all institutions. It feels reductive to have to point it out, but these events of summer 2020 must serve as a reminder to all that facile borders between diversity and institutional viability do more harm than good.

NOTES

1. Evren Odcikin and Rebecca Novick, "Who's In, Who's Out: The Numbers," *American Theatre Magazine*, April 10, 2019.

2. We See You, White American Theater, "About," www.weseeyouwat.com/about (accessed September 13, 2020).

3. We See You, White American Theater, "BIPOC Demands for White American Theatre," static1.squarespace.com/static/5ede42fd6cb927448d9d0525/t/5f064e63f21dd43ad 6ab3162/1594248809279/Tier2.pdf (accessed September 13, 2020).

Theater 51:1   DOI 10.1215/01610775-8824715

Tania El Khoury's
*Cultural Exchange
Rate*, LAB Biennial
*Where No Wall
Remains*, The
Fisher Center at
Bard, Annandale-
on-Hudson, NY,
2019. Photo: Maria
Baranova

TANIA EL KHOURY

CREATING INTIMACY AND CURATING BORDERS

As I write these words in Beirut, I feel my hands sinking into the keyboard. We just survived the biggest nonnuclear explosion in history. On August 4, 2020, 2,750 tons of ammonium nitrate exploded three miles away from our home. The blast destroyed half of the city, killing over two hundred people and injuring approximately seven thousand others, while at least fifty people remain missing. This was an extraordinary event that strangely feels familiar. Surviving in Lebanon is a familiar occurrence, and it is often in the company of equally crushing and familiar feelings: survivor's guilt, fear, anger, acute stress, and an obsession with revenge. I am unsure why this introduction is relevant to you, the reader of this text, other than the fact that it is a reality that needs to be shared between us, the reader and the writer. Sharing human vulnerability has been key to my art practice. Both my political motivations for making artwork and my chosen artistic form of interactive live art anchor my ethical and methodological commitments to create space for mutual vulnerability, intimacy, and care.

Before sitting down to write these words, I spent the first part of my day doing paperwork to secure my six-month-old daughter her first US passport and myself a US visa. Such bureaucratic forms seem to increase in precious value following a near-death or life-changing experience. In Beirut, conversations and debates about emigration, various border regimes, and seeking refuge have once again come to the fore among survivors—irrespective of how they or their loved ones were physically affected by the explosion. It seems only natural to feel the urge (and need) to move when an event—or series of developments—shreds their already fragile sense of security. Then again, borders can be as lethal as explosions. They too cause an incredible amount of suffering and death in our world. However, unlike explosions, borders kill and harm mostly in ways that are silent and invisible to those who choose not to know.

Borders have been a key thematic in my art practice in the last fifteen years, culminating thus far in cocurating with Gideon Lester the 2019 Live Arts Bard (LAB) Biennial *Where No Wall Remains* at Bard College in November 2019. If I were writ-

Theater 51:1   DOI 10.1215/01610775-8824729
© 2021 by Tania El Khoury

ing this text a decade ago, I would have confused my art practice with activism geared at sociopolitical change, without necessarily understanding what makes it function as such. Today, the world features even harsher border regimes: more discriminatory against and greater in their dispossession of unwanted bodies and increasingly accompanied with spectacular state violence. Since the Arab uprisings that started in 2010, we have witnessed mass displacement of people. Counterrevolutionary oppression has caused the dispossession of millions of people. Most ended up in neighboring countries; others, often the more affluent, ended up in Western countries. Some have reached their new locations through emigration processes and an asylum application on arrival. Others have put their lives at risk, hiring smugglers who lead them unto overcrowded and unreliable boats crossing a sea that has become a death trap. During the last decade we have witnessed some of the most discriminatory border policies in history. The rich world, which in many cases is responsible for the injustices that lead to displacement, whether by its colonial legacy or enabling of dictatorships, is committed to stopping the arrival of refugees by all means. The Australian government illegally held refugees in an offshore detention center on Manus Island, pushing a significant number of people to self-harm and attempt suicide. European countries initiated the Dublin Regulation that limits people's choices of travel by forcing them to remain where their fingerprints were first registered rather than where they would like to settle. Europe has also established Frontex, the controversial European Border and Coast Guard Agency, that functions with no transparency or accountability and that regularly breaks the law. Like ICE (Immigration and Customs Enforcement) in the United States, Frontex in Europe uses the tactic of deterrence against refugees rather than abiding by the human right of asylum and refuge. Governments have repeatedly demonized and criminalized their citizens who organize to help, support, and treat refugees with basic decency, solidarity, and humanity.

Although built on indigenous land by migrants and refugees, the United States of America has taken the fewest refugees from the Middle East this past decade. Additionally, Trump's Muslim ban was about limiting the travel of people from seven Muslim-majority countries and suspending the entry of Syrian refugees indefinitely. The United States held people in detention centers under inhumane conditions, even ripping children away from their families. The world has never seen such spectacularly harmful borders.

Today, I no longer conflate art with activism. I worry that if I do that I would be deceiving audiences and myself, all the while being self-congratulatory. The art I create or seek out has a political potential, yet this potentiality is not necessarily realized on the audience experiencing the artwork. The political potential is an aim we strive for, not an automatic result of everything we produce. It is an ongoing practice whose dynamic shifts with each and every work, and each and every instance of that work's presentation.

The art that I find inspiration in is not merely protest or action art, no matter how important these can be in intervening in everyday politics. I find inspiration in art that produces knowledge and exposes systems of oppression. These practices interrogate grand narratives and offer tools for resistance while sharing human vulnerability, empathy, and care. This type of art necessarily abides by the ethics and politics championed by its final form in the very process of creating that form.

While conceptualizing *Where No Wall Remains*, it felt crucial to curate artists rather than artworks. We wanted to invest resources, time, and energy in the art makers rather than in their outcomes. These artists have practiced border crossing in their work and in their everyday lives. Curating them was about learning from their experiences, listening to their voices, and engaging with their critical ideas. *Where No Wall Remains* consisted of nine commissioned pieces, giving the artists the opportunity to create new works and ourselves as curators the opportunity to witness that process unfold. The creation of the works materialized simultaneously in different parts of the world throughout 2019. The process culminated in a festival in New York that brought together various political contexts, artistic forms, and audience encounters—all of which connected together as one unifying event.

As an artist, I have presented my work in many festivals across the globe. Some of these festivals are a home away from home. Others are too awkward to recount. *Where*

Emilio Rojas's *m(Others): Hudson Valley*, LAB Biennial *Where No Wall Remains*, The Fisher Center at Bard, Annandale-on-Hudson, NY, 2019. Photo: Maria Baranova

No Wall Remains was my first time sitting at the curators' table, though I also created my own live art piece for the festival. Having the rare opportunity to cocurate, I set as one primary goal the creation of an experience for the other participating artists that I would myself appreciate at a festival. As an artist, I desire a festival that creates a community, that grants artists a space to grow, be critical, and be brave and to question their process and ethics. Additionally, I welcome a festival that centers on the experience of the audience not as consumers of artwork and merchandise but as cocreators and collaborators in the encounters with artists and artworks. Looking back at how *Where No Wall Remains* filled different spaces in the Fisher Center's building at Bard College, as well as overflowed into the nearby Bard Farm and the farther away Murray's Café in Tivoli, I remember groups of audience members engaging in conversations while being guided from one performance space to another. In the Frank Gehry–designed Fisher Center, we managed to create pockets of intimacy inside and outside the performance spaces. I recall audiences standing in hallways and sitting on benches between shows. They encountered artwork in the least obvious of spaces in this large building: corridors, storage spaces, and back stages. The audience regularly referred to the works they encountered as "experiences." We were deeply inspired and incredibly touched by the openness of everyone involved: artists, technicians, the festival team, and most important, the audience.

CREATING INTIMACY

I moved to London as a young college-educated adult to further pursue my art education. Upon arrival at the airport, a UK border officer sent me to a room. Therein, two people in gloves and masks performed a medical exam on me, intruding into my mouth and ears without ever giving any explanation. Before letting me through, another border officer told me that I should report to the police every time I change my home address. I ultimately refused to abide by this request so as to not contribute to the normalization of the criminalization of migrants. Remaining in London after my studies, I found myself producing work as an artist in an overwhelmingly white industry. The experience of racialization and the burden of representation that Black, Indigenous, and People of Color (BIPOC) artists are systematically subjected to greatly influenced my work. Like many, I experienced borders at every level: those between nation-states, cities as borders, the commodification of art as a border, and our bodies as borders. Perhaps the entirety of my art practice has always been about borders, whether physical or otherwise. For the sake of this text, I discuss only a small selection of these works. I explain how I chose to counter the violence of borders through intimate and interactive live art.

I begin with one of my most recent works, titled *As Far as My Fingertips Take Me* (2016). This is a one-to-one interactive piece between one audience member at a time

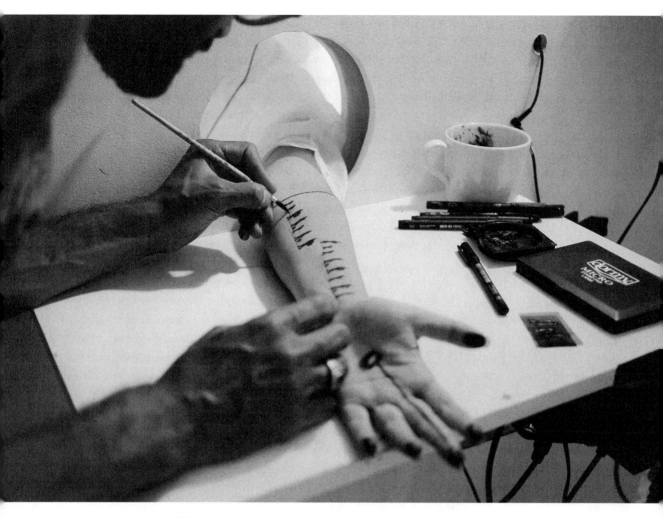

and one performer. The performer is the musician and street artist Basel Zaraa. Basel was born a Palestinian refugee in Yarmouk refugee camp in Damascus. He now lives in the United Kingdom, where we met and became both friends and collaborators. Like many of my works, *As Far as My Fingertips Take Me* is multisensory and immersive. This work is essentially a tactile and sound experience. The audience is invited to sit on one side of a white gallery wall and stick their left arm into a hole in the wall. On the other side, Basel is seated. He touches the audience's arm, massages it, and draws on it. While being marked by Basel, the audience listens through a pair of headphones to Basel's voice, first introducing himself, then narrating a story, and finally rapping a song that he created and recorded. *As Far as My Fingertips Take Me* was produced as a London International Festival of Theatre (LIFT) commission in partnership with the Royal Court Theatre. During our rehearsals, Basel and I joked that some privileged art goers may need to be literally touched by refugees to feel empathetic toward them. It

Tania El Khoury's *As Far as My Fingertips Take Me*, Fusebox Festival, Prizer Gallery, Austin, TX, 2018. Photo: Tania El Khoury was crucial for both Basel and me to counter the idea that the refugee "crisis" is a new phenomenon rather than an ongoing reality enforced by decades of wars and occupations, capitalist development, xenophobia, and securitized border politics.

The pristine white gallery wall between the audience and the performer was a physical border between two individuals at the same time that it was the art world as border. Can art really bring us closer? I imagined that many audiences will be reluctant to stick their arms in the hole and be touched by someone they could not see. We wanted to challenge them to be touched, seen, and rendered vulnerable. As tends to be the case, I was surprised by audiences. The response to this piece was overwhelming. People wanted to tour the work, talk about it, queue to see it, write articles and essays about it, invite Basel to family dinners, and commission us to work on another collaboration and sequel piece. The performance won a 2019 Bessie Award for Outstanding Production in New York. I often reflect on what made such a simple and short piece

Tania El Khoury and Dictaphone Group's *Nothing to Declare*, Ashkal Alwan, Beirut, Lebanon, 2013. Photo: Ramzy Haddad

remarkable for many people. I was told by some audiences that this was a ten-minute performance that remained with them for about four days. The drawings on the audiences' arms slowly disappeared with every wash. As such, their connection to that story, or perhaps to that cause, was constantly being questioned. Some audience members told us that they tried to keep the drawing on their arms for as long as possible, showering with a cover over their arm. A few even reached out to get permission to tattoo the drawing. I have so far seen one arm tattooed with the drawing from *As Far as My Fingertips Take Me*.

In 2009 I cofounded Dictaphone Group, a Beirut-based collective of research and live art. We worked on a number of pieces dealing with borders, the right of movement, and public space. *Nothing to Declare* (2013) explored both national and internal borders in Lebanon, many of which are invisible. I and my two collaborators, Abir Saksouk and Petra Serhal, each took a route following the disused train system until we reached the national border. Along the way we filmed abandoned stations, refugee camps, makeshift houses, military bases, and the accumulated traces of wars, occupations, and state violence. We shared our journey in a lecture performance that recounted the recent history of Lebanon through the use of train tracks and stations. This project produced fascinating research findings, based from collected oral histories and the study of the spaces we encountered. However, we were also producing a parallel research theme through the appearance of our bodies in formal and informal border zones. The physical act of crossing checkpoints and military zones and navigating homes, camps, and commercial places, all while simply following the train tracks and reaching national borders, ultimately proved to be a research practice in itself. We recorded these encounters between body and border both on film and in our notes—to later be shared with audiences. The appearance of our bodies exposed the menacing nature of borders. It was in fact borders themselves that rendered bodies vulnerable, as opposed to simply reflecting preexisting vulnerabilities.

A vast body of artwork on borders features images and scenes in which artists appear at a certain border and attempt to cross it, such as Anna Teresa Fernández's *Erasing the Border*, Richard Lou's *Border Door*, and Guadalupe Maravilla's *Crossing Performance*, to name a few. This type of work spans across symbolic, site-specific, durational, and action performance forms. It places art in direct confrontation with borders. However different in form and technique, these works set *at* borders *about* borders create a unique opportunity to challenge these frontiers. Borders bully us into acting within prescribed, standardized, and restrictive norms. On these man-made frontiers, we are supposed to perform our identities in an almost semichoreographed manner. We generally feel forced to put on our "best" performance, to appear as unthreatening as possible. We are reduced to our paperwork, accent, gender, race, and other markers of identities. For this reason, putting on an entirely different performance on borders, with its specifically designed visuals, movements, and vocabularies, disturbs the power structure of borders and irritates its official agents.

CULTURAL EXCHANGE RATE

In these instances of bodies against borders, the political potentiality of interactivity is apparent. Interactivity is thus a research and performance engine that is built on a two-way horizontal relationship between art and audience, artist and participant, art and passers-by, and art and artist. All the elements impact one another, feed into one another, and form a unique experience that can never be repeated in the same exact way.

The interactive installation performance I created as part of *Where No Wall Remains* has been in the making for several years. *Cultural Exchange Rate*, cocommissioned by Fisher Center at Bard in New York, Onassis Stegi in Athens, and Spielart Festival in Munich, does not take place on the site of a border but starts from it. The work employs interactivity both in the making process and in its encounter with the audience. In it, I share my family history with border crossings across a century. My family hails from a border village in Akkar, the northernmost region of Lebanon and considered by many the country's poorest region. The area suffered decades of state negligence, including a lack of basic infrastructure and social services. Our village gloriously overlooks another village, where many of its population are our blood relatives.

Tania El Khoury's
*Cultural Exchange
Rate*. Photo:
Maria Baranova

That neighboring village is in fact in another country, Syria. My fascination with natural unmarked borders first developed at an early age, from my own particular family history and from that hill that looks across the other hill in another country. In *Cultural Exchange Rate* I share that family history for the first time and tell stories spanning across a century of my family members' relationships with border crossing and migration. The content of the piece was collected through interviews with my late grandmother, a visit to Mexico City where I met lost relatives and searched for traces of my great grandfather, and documents and photographs shared by various family members. The audience is invited to enter a darkly lit space with two walls, each filled with secured metal cabinets that look like bank vaults or deposit boxes. Each audience is given a set of keys; each key opens a specific cabinet that the audience needs to stick their heads into so as to listen, watch, smell, see, touch, and/or taste. Every cabinet holds an entirely different scene, image, or material. Some cabinets follow my journey to Mexico and my quest for Mexican citizenship. Other cabinets focus on my family in Akkar and their relationship with migration and the river border. One cabinet takes the audience into a small room where they are invited to perform a currency exchange. These cabinets are experienced in different order by each audience member. Consequently, they each have a unique journey during this work. The content functions like a puzzle that audience members stitch together in their own way.

Although *Cultural Exchange Rate* functions as a performance, there are no performers in the piece. It features an audience guide and a team of technicians who freely enter the space when needed. It is the audience members themselves who perform the piece. They activate the space and transform an otherwise installation into a live event. The ten audience members work around each other, glance at each other, sometimes follow each other, other times wait for each other. Meanwhile, they each create their own journey and experience. Scale is an important element in the design of the piece. The actual space of the performance is relatively large; so are the cabinets that constitute the set. On the other hand, the audience members experience the work intimately, often only with their faces when they stick their heads into the various cabinets. It is almost as if the piece is theater for the head—the head here is not merely the brain but the gate that activates all senses. Inside the cabinet, the head is surrounded by a black fabric that shields it from the outside world. On both sides, next to the ears, hidden speakers broadcast sounds, music, or words—so close to the skin that sometimes they can feel the air moving. Close to their eyes they can watch a video or look at pictures or other objects in the cabinets. In one cabinet there are sweets that they can taste. In a number of cabinets smell constitutes an element of storytelling. The intimacy of these microexperiences works in juxtaposition with the coldness of bank vaults and the theme of political economy.

Tania El Khoury's *Cultural Exchange Rate*. Photo: Maria Baranova

Like *As Far as My Fingertips Take Me*, the chosen form of *Cultural Exchange Rate* is an opportunity to be self-critical of the role and limits of art in evoking empathy. Do we really need to open one another's closets and stick our heads in a family's intimate stories and lives to understand what makes people migrate? I am not sure. Though I now know that being immersed in other realities offers an opportunity not only for the audience to feel empathy but also to evoke their own stories, memories, and feelings on the subject.

When we opened *Cultural Exchange Rate* in November 2019, Lebanon seemed hopeful with the spark of a mass uprising that erupted on October 17 of that year. The country was definitely not suffering as badly as it is right now. Its economy was threatened but nowhere near collapsed as it currently is. Its currency was not depreciating precipitously to stabilize at 20 percent of its original value. This is without mentioning the brutal state repression of protests followed by the devastating explosion this August. Today, once again, large groups of people are migrating from Lebanon, trying to survive its economic collapse and lack of security. Just like my great-grandfather did nearly a century ago, the youngest members of my family are now looking at migration as their only means of survival and (perhaps) growth. *Cultural Exchange Rate* is currently loaded with a sense of heaviness and sadness that was not present last year. Such is the nature of interactive work: they transform and adapt, and sometimes carry entirely new meanings.

CURATING THE VIOLENCE OF BORDERS

Where No Wall Remains hosted nine total works of various media: video, live music, dance theater, live art, visual art, and interactive installations and performances. All these works were new, as they were commissioned by the festival. As cocurators, Gideon Lester and I watched them come to life for the first time during dress rehearsals. We were in complete awe about how special each of the works felt but also how they communicated with one another in various layers of meaning and politics. Some of these pieces centered the personal within the political, putting the artist-narrator's body in the context of navigating a border. This is particularly poignant in Emily Jacir's powerful video *Letter to a Friend*. Therein the artist documents the everyday struggles and tear gas attacks on her street and home in Bethlehem. In *Fito*, Rudi Goblen tells a story of his "naturalization" process in a stylish concert that leaves us wanting to move with him while at the same time feeling the responsibility of bearing witness to immigrant lives in the United States. The artists' own stories and positionality vis-à-vis their research are apparent even in the most poetic of pieces. In *At These Terrifying Frontiers Where the Existence and Disappearance of People Fade into Each Other*, Basel Abbas and Ruanne Abou-Rahme in collaboration with the sound and image performance group

Tashweesh take us on an audiovisual journey of erasure, disruption, and disappearances of bodies that stubbornly end up appearing again. Mirna Bamieh (of the Palestine Hosting Society live art project), in *Menu of Dis/Appearance*, does a similar process of unearthing herbs, food culture, and elements that were being forced into erasure and disappearance by the Israeli occupation. These pieces, along with my own *Cultural Exchange Rate* and Emilio Rojas's *Naturalized Borders (to Gloria)*, place the audience at the center of the work, making them collaborators in the event but also witnesses of these various appearances and disappearances along borders. Another work by Emilio Rojas, *m(Others): Hudson Valley*, is an installation of local immigrant women holding their first-generation US children. The mothers are hidden under a fabric in the style of 1920s studio photography where mothers hide while carrying their children be photographed. In this project, Rojas challenges the racist narrative that erases the labor of immigrant mothers and reduces their connection to their children to simply seeking US residency.

Two artworks I think of in particular relation to each other are Ali Chahrour's *Night* dance performance and Jason De León's interactive installation *Hostile Terrain 94*, perhaps because they both occupied the center part of Fisher Center, with *Night* happening in the theater while *Hostile Terrain 94* literally grew throughout the festival on the wall facing the theater. Ali's previous trilogy was about death, mourning rituals, and lamentation. *Night* is the beginning of his trilogy about love, but somehow death is also present in *Night* in the many borders we place on love and on the body. *Hostile Terrain 94* documents the deaths of people crossing the Arizona-Mexico border, yet somehow the piece has a lot of love in it: the love of the team who worked on this documentary installation, paying respect to every person who fell victim to border discrimination and violence; the love of the families who shared information about their deceased loved ones; and the love of participating audience members who filled in (by hand) the 3,117 toe tags with the death details of those who died attempting to migrate.

Where No Wall Remains aimed to be an event with political capacity, rather than yet another festival on migration. For me, it succeeded in doing so in two ways. First, we were conscious that the debate should not only center on the resilience of the "good" migrant and refugee but also address borders as violence, which connects the right to movement with the responsibility and positionality of people who are border privileged, those who are not criminalized for crossing borders. Second, in terms of form, the festival created spaces of interactivity, intimacy, and connection, hence placing the audience inside these realities and stories, inviting them to embody that knowledge and allowing them space and time for conversation and political transformation. Both of these aspects were facilitated by the selection of artists who work with multiple senses and in multidisciplinary forms. The work of the Palestine Hosting Society, for example, employs taste, smell, and touch. This live art project's works take the form of a gather-

Tania El Khoury's
*Cultural Exchange
Rate.* Photo: Maria
Baranova

ing around a dinner table, building a temporary community that breaks bread together and that connects the audience with the content of the research through the experience of their body before their rationality. Similarly, the work of Emilio Rojas brought the audience to the farm to experience his land art. His work connected various communities with one another: the locals, the visitors, the migrants, and the Indigenous. Just like the land where the work existed, different layers of crops and different layers of meaning leaned over one another and formed the experience of the work. Rojas invited the audience to remember a border that they haven't necessarily seen or crossed. The act of remembrance here is an act of redrawing the border and reimagining it perhaps in a way that leaves it compromised or even wide open.

CONCLUSION

Writing this text from Beirut in the aftermath of one the most spectacular moments of state violence that we have encountered in our already eventful lives, I feel the urge for revenge and destruction. There is no violence more harmful and lethal than state violence. Today, it feels particularly challenging to connect political rage with an art form that is subtle, intimate, and caring. However, it is necessary for us to remember that we owe it to ourselves and our audiences to practice mutual care. It seems particularly crucial to view our audiences as allies or allies to be. For we have nothing left other than our solidarity and a sense of radical care and love that counters state violence. Working collaboratively, employing interactivity and intimacy, and sharing vulnerability have kept many of us hopeful about an art practice that functions as collectivism. This way of working is becoming more essential in the current political climate. It is currently difficult to imagine a postpandemic world with busy and intimate festivals and other events, yet perhaps it is exactly what we should be aiming for: a stronger connection, solidarity, and collectivism. We come together intimately not to be an exclusive homogeneous group but to challenge one another to practice the politics we strive for in this world.

Jason De León's
Hostile Terrain 94,
LAB Biennial *Where
No Wall Remains*,
The Fisher Center
at Bard, Annandale-
on-Hudson, NY,
2019. Photo: Maria
Baranova

Portfolio

HOSTILE TERRAIN 94

Jason De León
Introduction by Gabriel Canter

Started in 2009, the Undocumented Migration Project (UMP) is a long-term anthropological study of clandestine movement between Latin America and the United States that uses ethnography, archaeology, visual anthropology, and forensic science to understand this violent social process and raise awareness through research, education, and public outreach.

By combining ethnographic work in Mexico with forensic and archaeological research in Arizona, the UMP has improved our knowledge of this highly politicized and poorly understood process and demonstrated how an archaeological approach can provide new insight into a contemporary social phenomenon. The research being conducted by the UMP is interdisciplinary, a fact reflected by the project's diverse theoretical and methodological approaches, the wide range of venues where this work is being published, and the ethnographic-archaeological field school that has been running in Arizona and Mexico since 2010. Some of the work of the UMP has been on display through traveling exhibitions, such as *State of Exception/Estado de Excepción* (2013–17) and *Hostile Terrain 94* (2019–). *Hostile Terrain 94* was presented at the *Where No Wall Remains* Live Arts Bard (LAB) Biennial of the Fisher Center at Bard College in the fall of 2019, and it is that presentation that is documented in the following pages.

In 1994, the US Border Patrol implemented the immigration enforcement strategy known as "prevention through deterrence" (PTD). This was a policy designed to discourage undocumented migrants from attempting to cross the US-Mexico border near

Theater 51:1 DOI 10.1215/01610775-8824743

urban ports of entry. With these traditional crossing points closed off, it was expected that people would then attempt to cross the border illegally in more remote and depopulated regions on foot, where the natural environment would act as a physical deterrent. It was anticipated that the difficulties people experienced while traversing dozens of miles across what the Border Patrol deemed the "hostile terrain" of places like the Sonoran Desert of Arizona would eventually discourage migrants from attempting the journey. This strategy failed to stop border crossers, and instead, more than 6 million people have attempted to migrate into the United States through the Sonoran Desert of southern Arizona since the mid-1990s. At least thirty-two hundred people have died, largely from dehydration and hyperthermia, while attempting this journey through Arizona. In recent years this policy has shifted people toward Texas, where hundreds (if not thousands) have perished while attempting to cross the border in that region. PTD is still the primary border enforcement strategy being used along the US-Mexico border today.

Hostile Terrain 94 is a participatory art exhibition created by the UMP, directed by UCLA anthropologist Jason De León. This installation is intended to raise awareness about the realities of the US-Mexico border, focusing on the deaths that have been happening almost daily since 1994 as a direct result of PTD.

The installation depicts a map wall that contains 3117 toe tags representing people who have died while crossing the US-Mexico border between the mid-1990s and 2020. Manila tags represent people who have been identified. Orange tags represent unidentified human remains. The construction of this memorial is realized with the help of local volunteers who have handwritten the information of the dead. These tags are then placed on the map in the exact location where those remains were found. The physical act of writing out the names and information for the dead invites participants to reflect, witness, and stand in solidarity with those who have lost their lives in search of a better one. Several toe tags on the wall have QR codes that connect to online content regarding migrant issues along the southern US border.

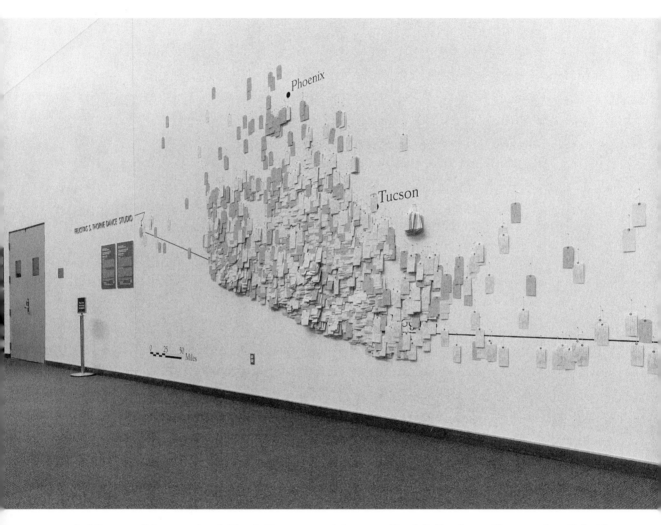

A full view of the completed *Hostile Terrain 94* exhibition at Bard College's LAB Biennial. Over the course of one week, students and community members came together to fill out handwritten toe tags representing the thousands who have died and disappeared in the Sonoran Desert of southern Arizona as a result of US Border Patrol's 1994 policy of "prevention through deterrence."

Jason De León's *Hostile Terrain 94*. Photo: Maria Baranova

3117 toe tags hang on a map wall, each representing someone who lost their life crossing the us-Mexico border. Each tag is in the same geolocation where that individual's body was found. Lighter tags represent identified individuals, and darker tags represent unidentified human remains.

Jason De León's
*Hostile Terrain
94*. Photo: Maria
Baranova

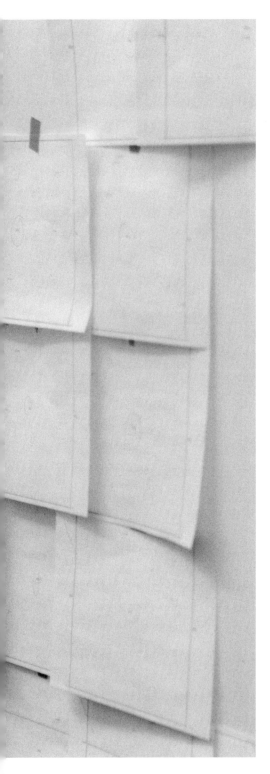

Cocurator Michael Wells installs tags onto the *Hostile Terrain 94* wall just before the opening at Bard College's LAB Biennial.

Jason De León's *Hostile Terrain 94*. Photo: Maria Baranova

Volunteers fill out toe tags with death details of the more than thirty-one hundred people who have died while crossing the Sonoran Desert of southern Arizona. The process of handwriting each individual's name causes the volunteer to directly engage with this information and reflect on the harsh realities of us border policies.

As participants fill out toe tags, they often engage in conversations with each other, even if they begin the session as strangers. Grappling with the emotional task of writing all of the information tends to elicit a reaction to talk with those nearby, as a kind of coping mechanism.

Jason De León's
Hostile Terrain
94. Photo: Maria
Baranova

Viewers read names of the individuals who have perished at the hands of US Border Patrol policies, such as "prevention through deterrence." Standing up close, one can feel the weight of all thirty-one hundred tags hanging from their pins on the map.

Jason De León's *Hostile Terrain 94.* Photo: Maria Baranova

Volunteers who fill out tags are welcome to write a personal message on the backs of the tags, and viewers are able to get an up-close view.

Jason De León's
*Hostile Terrain
94.* Photo: Maria
Baranova

Some tags on the wall have QR codes that viewers can scan to connect to online content, to interact with various augmented reality components regarding migrant issues along the southern US border.

Jason De León's *Hostile Terrain 94*. Photo: Maria Baranova

Ali Chahrour's
Night, LAB Biennial
*Where No Wall
Remains*, The
Fisher Center at
Bard, Annandale-
on-Hudson, NY,
2019. Photo: Maria
Baranova

ALI CHAHROUR

NIGHT

The Catastrophe is a violent crisis during which the subject, experiencing the amorous situation as a
definitive impasse, a trap from which he can never escape, sees himself doomed to total destruction.
—Roland Barthes, *A Lover's Discourse: Fragments*

Night is a performance that draws inspiration from the prolific themes of love and
romance in classical Arabic poetry, recounting stories of lovers and their cruel separa-
tions.

The work references tales from the memory of the Levant and Mesopotamia, as
well as more contemporary stories about the fate of lovers who challenged social and
religious structures, trying to break the walls of segregation—lovers who are stuck in
"the Catastrophe," as Barthes wrote, whose bodies are punished, sentenced to a life
between the desire for separation and the impossible hope of reunion.

The performance documents the alternations of lovers and their resistance, up
until the point of their collapse, when they fade away. The exhausted body succumbs,
and every movement, every instrument it has carried drops with it. That fall exposes
the fragility of the lover/performer and the frail nature of methods and tools. The stage
transforms into a battlefield, one where the battle has ended and on which the audience
has just witnessed the end or, rather, the birth of its heroes.

Night eclipses the borders of religion, race, and gender. It questions the essence
of love and the intimacy of existing amid the hate of contemporary societies. It explores
the meaning of a body's limits and the curbing of its desires, drawing an emotional
map that may punish those who trespass it, just as geographical borders would. It is as
though love had its own map, fortified with the barbed wires that defend its borders.
They kill the lover trying to flee and punish the lover getting caught in their trap. They
are the borders of bodies, feelings, and desires, and they are equally defined by politics.
It shapes love and fits it into molds that resemble transit visas. *Night* tries to observe
society and its constituents by exploring modern stories of love, as well as the classical

Theater 51:1   DOI 10.1215/01610775-8824757
© 2021 by Yale School of Drama/Yale Repertory Theatre

tales passed down from one generation to the next. It unfolds the political, religious, and social complexities that influence the fate of relationships, their intimacy, and the role of the body.

The performance references a number of sources from different time periods, including most notably *Masare' Al Ishshaq* (*Deaths of Lovers*, first published in 1907 AD/1325 AH), a book in which the writer Abi Mohamed Jaafar Ben Ahmad Bin Hussein Al-Seraj Al-Qaree (known as Al-Seraj Al-Qaree) collected all the stories he found of lovers who were consumed by their passion and died of love. Within its pages are stories of people on their deathbed, in the throes of agony, uttering poetry as they surrender their last breath. One chapter of his book mentions the last moments of the life of the poet, and another talks of a lover from the time he met the object of his affection until the moment he died for it.

The book also tells the story of Mohamed Bin Daoud. His father, Daoud Bin Ali (known as Daoud Al-Zahiri) was an Iraqi Muslim scholar and the founder of a school of Islamic jurisprudence characterized by its reliance on the manifest (*zahir*) meaning of expressions in the Quran and Hadiths, and its rejection of analogical deduction and interpretation. His son's genius was quickly revealed as he memorized the Quran

Ali Chahrour's *Night*. Photo: Maria Baranova

by heart and displayed supernatural intelligence. Upon his father's death, Mohamed Bin Daoud took his place as a jurist, issuing *fatwas* (rulings on Islamic law) despite his young age and soon leading the clerics in Baghdad and Iraq. Mohamed Bin Daoud was said to be enamored with a youth from Isfahan, a certain Mohamed Bin Jamea, who was known to lavish and spend on Bin Daoud—so much so that it was said, "Never was seen a loved one who spent so much on he who loves him."

One day, Mohamed Bin Jamea, upon seeing his reflection in the mirror, was pleased with his beauty. He quickly covered his face with a veil and went to Mohamed Bin Daoud thus attired. Bin Daoud asked him, "What is this?" And Bin Jamea answered, "I saw myself in the mirror and was pleased by my beauty, and I did not want anyone else to see it before you." Mohamed Ben Daoud swooned from an excess of passion.

The story is thus recounted in *Al-Wafi Bil Wafiyat*, by Salah El Dine Khalil Bin Aybak Al Safadi, and in *Masare' Al Ishshaq* by Al-Seraj Al-Qaree:

> It was said that in one of Mohamed Ben Daoud's assemblies a man asked him (in verse):
>> Oh Bin Daoud, oh scholar of Iraq,
>> Advise us on killer gazes
>> Are their wounds to be punished?
>> Or is the bleeding of lovers allowed?

Bin Daoud answered:

> How could a man advise you who is perishing by the arrows of separation
> and longing?

For Bin Daoud, better the death of a reunion, than death by separation.

Mohamed Bin Daoud remained in love with Bin Jamea until his death. It is said he was visited at his deathbed and was asked, "How may we relieve you?" and he answered, "The love of you know whom has led me to this," indicating his love for Bin Jamea.

In addition to *Masare' Al Ishshaq*—which is a treasure trove of recorded stories of lovers, with all their political, religious, and social entanglements—we also relied on the love stories of people for whom hearts have beaten and whose voices have inflamed passions, such as Iraqi performer Nazem al-Ghazali and his wife Salima Murad, and Al-Qasabji and Umm Kulthum, as well as contemporary stories from our modern world that we found and archived.

In exploring the modern aesthetics of love, in the classic stories inherited from love, and in their relationships with our contemporary society lies the importance of revisiting this rich and intense heritage, as well as its aesthetics. *Night* explores them with modern tools and thorough theoretical research that stems from a solid foundation. It creates the tools for local contemporary dance that questions the body's presence and its problems in relation to the collective memory, the heritage, and the components of our society. The performance reconsiders the scale of the violence and repression that are imposed on the methods of expressing love, of molding it, and of defining its rules. In Iraq, the Abbasid jurist Muhammad ibn Dawud once wrote poetry for his lover. Today he kills and abuses the bodies of lovers, merely because of their choices that went beyond religious and social boundaries.

Night begins with an exploration of the origin of the word: its aesthetics alongside the definitions of love in Arabic language and culture. It is an exploration of all that the word carries: an exploration of the state of lovers and their feelings, of their sadness, their joy, and their poetry. Most of all, it is an exploration of their freedoms:

> And in love there is desire and disease, there are the seeds and the bubbles of a pool
> in rain, there is the stability of one who is anchored, there is agitation and turmoil,
> for it is the reunion of lovers, the fruit's edible core and its root. It is rush, yearning,
> ardor, adoration, emotion, passion, intimate exchange, longing, exhaustion, sur-
> render, then affection, harmony, adulation, frenzy.
>
> The flame, the heat, the tenderness, the intensity, the devotion, the fever,
> the delirium, the intoxication, the whims, the trials and tribulations, the dread,
> the sadness, the anxiousness, the depression, the sting, the burn, the sleeplessness, the
> insomnia, the envy, the nostalgia, the pangs, the madness, the bewilderment, the
> straying, the spreading malady, the intimacy, the enslavement, the enthrallment,
> the affliction.

Ali Chahrour's
Night. Photo: Maria
Baranova

Ali Chahrour's
Night. Photo: Maria
Baranova

The nostalgia, the desire, the melancholy, the adulation, the embrace, the fervor, the companionship, the familiarity, the infatuation.

The suffering, the adoration, the intensity, the veneration, the ecstasy, the ardor.

The burn, the dread, the irony, the insanity, the sting, the torment, the bitterness, the love.

The passion, the heart, the lust, the craving, the suffering, the outburst, the pining, the sleeplessness, the insomnia, the intoxication, the patience, the seed, the core, the slaughter, the drowning, the fragrance, the thirst, the rot, the yearning, the adulation, the madness.

Al-junun is madness, a state of love

Al-jun is dissimulation

and from it *al-janeen* the fetus that remains unseen in the belly

Jan aleihi al-leil, the night unleashed its madness upon him, the night hid him in its darkness. From it comes *al-djinn*, the spirits that are hidden and invisible

and from it also *janan*, the grave and the shroud.

Junna anka, what was hidden from you.

Al-jannu and *al-junun* of the night, its darkness and dimness.

The ground when it is maddened *junnat* and *tajannanat*, it blossoms and from it emerges heaven (*janna*)

And *al-janan* dissimulated in the chest is the heart . . .

Ali Chahrour's
Night. Photo: Maria
Baranova

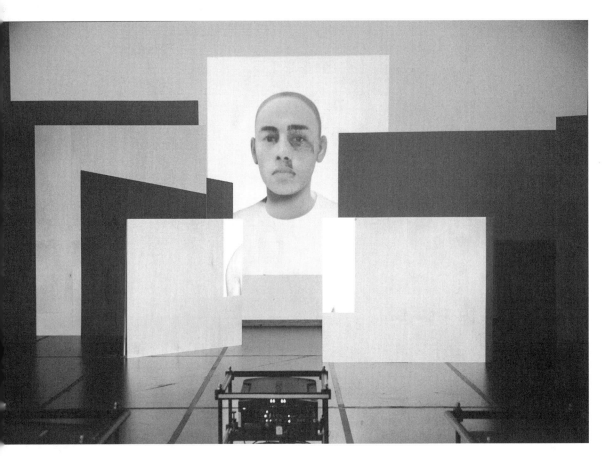

Basel Abbas
and Ruanne
Abou-Rahme's
*At those terrifying
frontiers where
the existence and
disappearance of
people fade into each
other (part 2)*, LAB
Biennial *Where No
Wall Remains*, The
Fisher Center at
Bard, Annandale-
on-Hudson, NY,
2019. Photo:
Maria Baranova

BASEL ABBAS AND RUANNE ABOU-RAHME

IF ONLY THIS MOUNTAIN BETWEEN US COULD BE GROUND

At those terrifying frontiers where the existence and disappearance of people fade into each other (part 2) is a site-specific video and sound installation by Basel Abbas and Ruanne Abou-Rahme featuring a new performance by the sound and image performance group Tashweesh, an improvised constellation that brings the artists together with musician/performer Muqata'a. Tashweesh combines their different practices in a joint performance, using sound, music, and image. The result is an exploration of the collision between sound and video, field recordings, archival material, vocals, breaks, and soundscapes.

The installation and performance are centered on recent projects by Abbas and Abou-Rahme that think about an expanded idea of returns: from the returns of the land and stubborn vegetation that does not die, to artifacts that are reactivated as living matter, figures that return in virtual form, and disruptive bodies that keep reappearing on borders, in feeds. Both the installation and performance deal with the intentional erosion of bodies in different forms, actual and virtual bodies, land/ecology and built structures, as well as their reappearance and return in spaces where they "should not be." These projects come together in a live setting, inviting us to consider the forms of entanglement between the destruction of bodies and the erasure of images, and the conditions under which these same bodies and images might once again reappear.

At those terrifying frontiers . . . weaves fragments from Edward Said's most personal and poetic work, *After the Last Sky*, and repurposes them to create a new script that reflects on what it means now to be constructed as an "illegal" person, body, or entity. The script is turned into a song sung by the artists as multiple avatars. Using software that generates avatars from a single image, the avatars in the video are all people who participated in the "March of Return" that continues to take place on the seamline in Gaza, an area that has been under physical siege since 2006. The relation-

Theater 51:1   DOI 10.1215/01610775-8824771

Basel Abbas
and Ruanne
Abou-Rahme's
*At those terrifying
frontiers . . .* Photo:
Maria Baranova

ships among fugitivity, fragility, and futurity become manifest in this field. The project uses low-resolution images that were circulated online, and the avatar software renders the missing data and information in the original image as scars, glitches, and incomplete features on the characters faces.

Oh shining star testify is structured around CCTV footage taken from an Israeli military surveillance camera. On March 19, 2014, fourteen-year-old Yusef Shawamreh crossed the "separation fence" erected by the Israeli military near Hebron. He was going to pick *akub*, an edible plant that is a delicacy in Palestinian cuisine, which blooms for only a short period of time and grows at high altitudes. After Yusef crossed the fence, Israeli forces ambushed him and shot him dead. A court injunction forced the military surveillance footage to be released, which was consequently circulated online, only to be removed later.

Oh shining star testify weaves together a fragmented script sampled from online

Basel Abbas and Ruanne Abou-Rahme's *Oh shining star testify*, LAB Biennial *Where No Wall Remains*, The Fisher Center at Bard, Annandale-on-Hudson, NY, 2019. Photo: Maria Baranova

Basel Abbas
and Ruanne
Abou-Rahme's
*And yet my mask
is powerful*, LAB
Biennial *Where No
Wall Remains*, The
Fisher Center at
Bard, Annandale-
on-Hudson, NY,
2019. Video still.
Courtesy of Basel
Abbas and Ruanne
Abou-Rahme

recordings of everyday erasures of bodies, land, and built structures, as well as their reappearance through ritual and performance. Moments from this material appear as moving layers with images building in density on top of each other, obscuring what came before in an accumulation of constant testament and constant erasure, retriev-ing, in this unfolding accumulation and dissipation of testament, certain moments that have passed us by as noise, what we cannot turn to see and what we cannot turn away from. Uncounted bodies counter their own erasures, appearing on a street, on a link, on a feed.

And yet my mask is powerful confronts the apocalyptic imaginary and the violence that dominates our contemporary moment. Taking Adrienne Rich's poem "Diving into the Wreck" as the beginnings of a script, *And yet my mask is powerful* asks what happens to people/places/things/materials when a living fabric is destroyed. The project uses the trips taken by young Palestinians to the sites of their destroyed villages inside Israel as an avatar for rethinking the site of the wreckage. In these returns the site of wreck-age becomes the very material from which to trace the faint contours of another pos-sible time. Something strange happens in these returns. The destroyed sites not only emerge as places of ruin or trauma but appear full of an unmediated vitality. The young people making these trips treat the sites as a living fabric. They reactivate the disused spaces, camp out onsite, eat, sing, dance. But even more, something in the very tissue of the site itself is undeniably living and resisting colonial erasures. It permeates from the soil into the stone and back into every bit of vegetation. There is a swarm of nonhuman life forces here, from the insects to the wild thorns, to the pomegranate trees that are inscribed with the living memory and story of the site. And it is here in the living archive of the vegetation itself that the site lives and breathes.

In its intersections between performativity and ritual, body and artifact, thingness and virtuality, *And yet my mask is powerful* begins to splice together a countermythology to the dominant mythologies of the present. The layers of images, texts, sound, and things perform and activate various forms of returns, flash-forwards, and déjà vu, unfolding in this gesture a dense story of erasures and reappearances, dispossession and resistance.

Basel Abbas and Ruanne Abou-Rahme's *At those terrifying frontiers . . .* Photo: Maria Baranova

LIVE ARTS BARD 2019 BIENNIAL
WHERE NO WALL REMAINS
حيث لا جدار يبقى
DONDE NO QUEDA NINGÚN MURO

MIRNA BAMIEH
PALESTINE HOSTING SOCIETY   إستضافات فلسطين
MENU OF DIS/APPEARANCE   عشاء التواري

November 21-23, 2019 | Murray's, Tivoli

MOUNEH

Wine Pairing: Chenin Blanc Viognier

A selection of in-house pickles
pickled turnips, mixed pickled salad of cauliflower, cucumbers, carrots, and chilis, green olives

Gaza-Style Dukka with olive oil

Shatta
preserved red hot chili pepper paste

Taboon and Kmaj bread

BREAKING BREAD

Khobz smeedeh
yellow bread stuffed with wheat and cinnamon

APPETIZERS

Wine Pairing: M.A.N. Family Wines Shiraz

Shroushat roots salad
fennel root, fennel leaves, dill, radish, raisins, pickled red onions, pickles hibiscus flowers, mint leaves, and pine leaves-infused olive oil vinaigrette

Rummaniyeh/Habbet Rumman
brown lentils, eggplant, pomegranate juice, molasses, and tahini, topped with pomegranate seeds and caramelized onions

Msalwa'a
lentil and rice porridge, topped with ferments and crunchy Freekeh, smoked green wheat

Kubbeh Niyyeh Majdalawieh
minced meat with bulgur, seasoned with red bell pepper paste
accompanied by Hashweh
cooked chopped lamb, onion, and pine nuts

MAINS

Wine Pairing: Barone Fini Merlot

Maftoul (vegetarian option available)
pumpkin, onion, chickpeas and chicken stew
served with Tasqiya
dill seeds, onion, chili and lime

Red Carrots
stuffed with rice, meat, and pine nuts, cooked in tamarind sauce – vegan variation stuffed with rice, chickpeas, and pine nuts

DESSERT

Gazan Arabieh Knafeh
bulgur with walnuts, pistachios, and cinnamon with orange blossom sugar syrup

Orange Sorbet
inspired by olive-picking season, drizzled of olive oil and wheat crumble

DRINKS

Hibiscus Natural Soda *with orange blossom and cloves*

White Coffee *cardamom and orange blossom*

Menu from Palestine Hosting Society's *Menu of Dis/Appearance*, LAB Biennial *Where No Wall Remains*, Murray's, Tivoli, NY, 2019. Courtesy of The Fisher Center at Bard

Menu of Dis/Appearance

Mirna Bamieh, interviewed by Gideon Lester

Palestine Hosting Society, a live art project that explores traditional food culture in Palestine, emphasizes dishes on the verge of disappearing under occupation. Some have been forgotten, their names now an abstraction to a younger generation of Palestinians. Over dinner tables, on walks, and through public interventions, the Palestine Hosting Society brings them back to life while also reflecting on the conditions that characterize Palestinian communities today, including border policies restricting food and water resources and wild plant foraging. Walls, checkpoints, and other militarized barriers dividing Palestinian regions complicate the regular sourcing of ingredients; without them, some traditional cuisine is already disappearing from daily life.

Menu of Dis/Appearance, *Palestine Hosting Society's first dinner performance in the United States, was presented in November 2019 at the Live Arts Bard (LAB) Biennial* Where No Wall Remains, *bringing together dishes from Palestinian cities and villages, as well refugee camps outside Palestine, while narrating stories about time, history, and intergenerational food habits that may be slipping away. Cocurator Gideon Lester spoke with artist and chef Mirna Bamieh in spring 2020 to reflect on the platform she founded and on performances celebrating food in the context of dispossession.—Ed.*

GIDEON LESTER: *Your current work focuses on fermentation. Of all the areas of cuisine and your practice you could focus on, why fermentation?*

MIRNA BAMIEH: I'm creating an artist cookbook—a novel cookbook—about fermentation. The character (the artist, I call her) reflects on everything through the fermentation process, and then there are recipes. There's a text, like a short story, and then the recipe that goes hand in hand with the text. It's a project that I started last year, but during COVID I've been focused on it more. Part of it will be in a show in Warsaw next year, and the final book will be published in 2022.

It was an aspect that I wanted to go into deeper. When I started, a whole world opened for me and now I'm passionate about the bacterial world and yeast. At the beginning of the pandemic, the first thing I was doing was building my pantry and thinking of preservation and creating sustainable food practices. Fermentation is one of them. It's the most diverse one because you stretch the taste and life of fresh produce and build sustainability with flavor in your kitchen. Each culture tells its own story through fermentation. I was just discussing with my father today how there's one ferment for each country that all other countries look down upon. I'm preparing a fermented yogurt with chopped lemon, and

Theater 51:1 DOI 10.1215/01610775-8824785

Palestine Hosting Society's *Menu of Dis/Appearance*, LAB Biennial *Where No Wall Remains*, Murray's, Tivoli, NY, 2019. Photo: Maria Baranova

lemon juice, and chilies, and fenugreek seeds. It's the Gazan version of it, but the original one, the Egyptian one, needed to ferment for years. They say that to eat this ferment, you have to take out the ants. It's so strong, but all Egyptians love it. Some ferments are very cultural. You grow to like them somehow.

Because we're all locked down for the pandemic, it feels like we are being fermented as well, so it was the perfect timing for me to reflect and approach time in a different way. Each ferment needs a certain time to mature.

Is there a political dimension to fermentation? Does it carry coded meaning for you?

It can. When you think of sustainability and self-sovereignty, and how you can take care of your family without relying on external factors that choose when to give you food or not to give you food, it can be political in that sense. Palestine Hosting Society is a way for me to

learn the wisdom of our grandfathers and grandmothers that was mostly interrupted for political reasons because of the loss of the land and because they couldn't have control and access to their food resources. For me it's a way of learning how our ancestors would deal with times of scarcity. Now we are living in a time when we don't know if we will have all the resources we are used to having. We cannot even move as freely as we used to before. It's this mental space that I want to learn, to reclaim. With that, you gain access to your own body, your own home, your own country, your own life.

How did you come to found Palestine Hosting Society?

I was producing mostly video installations from 2009 until 2017, when I started Palestine Hosting Society. Until 2016 I was focused on understanding what disappearance means.

If we abstracted the land, what is left from the Palestinian identity? Or if we abstracted memory, what does it mean to forget? For me it was based on disappearance. The first video installation I did in 2009 was a white map of nothingness, a map of disappearance imposed on the space. In works after that, I was looking into disappearing landscapes, disappearing memories, asking, What happens when your body disappears, what is left of you?

In 2016 there was a shift in the way I dealt with life and art. I started a live art project called Potato Talks focused on storytelling in public squares in Ramallah, Jerusalem, and other cities. The first one was in Marrakech, Morocco. I was working with other people changing the space of the square through stories. I realized that the artwork I love creates an ephemeral experience with an audience that you do not expect. I went to Tokyo after that and realized that what I love in the world, as much as art, is food. I really can tell the story of my life through my experience with different foods. So I took what I thought would be a break: I went to culinary school. But midway through my studies I realized that

actually those two can be brought together in a nice way, and that's how Palestine Hosting Society was born. It started in people's houses, because this whole project is a learning space for me as much as it's a creation of knowledge and a sharing of knowledge.

So the audience for the earliest Palestine Hosting Society events, performances, dinners were other Palestinians?

Yes. And even now, whenever there is a table happening here, I make sure that it's in Arabic because I want to target Palestinian audiences. Because the food research and the dishes I present on those tables are not really familiar dishes for the Palestinians. They're almost forgotten dishes. And if the dish is familiar, then this story that I bring to the table for that dish is something that I want people to be more aware of. The links I create between intimate histories and geographies and how we can read our present moment through those dishes and food practices are something that needs to be highlighted in Palestine.

Palestine Hosting Society's *Menu of Dis/Appearance.* Photo: Maria Baranova

If a dish has been forgotten, what form does your research take? How do you discover it and reconstruct it? What is the archive for you?

There are different levels of forgetting and disappearance. One dish can be totally forgotten in one area, but in another it might remain preserved in the memories of the mothers or grandmothers. Or maybe just one woman will remember this dish. For my research, I just meet people and ask them questions. When I was working on wild edible plants, I would go to different regions in Palestine to meet people. We'd take walks and they'd remember for me, with me, while we're walking, while we're looking at plants in the mountains. Sometimes I ask them, and sometimes I tell them what I know, and then they want to teach me more. They remember things that they didn't even think that they still remembered. So it's very spontaneous, but somehow I lead people into remembering. And then we cook together.

You work fairly often with dishes from Gaza, which presumably presents special difficulties for you since you can't go there.

One of the main reasons recipes are being forgotten in Palestine is because, physically, Palestinians cannot move freely from place to place. There's a real rupture between Palestinians in the West Bank and Palestinians living in Jerusalem, and Palestinians living in Galilee, and Palestinians living in Gaza. Physical restraints make people not know what the others cook, and therefore the whole Palestinian cuisine is reduced to a few main dishes. Although *rummanieh, sayyadieh, fugga'iya* are regional, not all of Palestine would cook it. I have a Jerusalem ID, so I can go to Galilee and Jerusalem, unlike other Palestinians. It's a temporary residency, but at least I have access. But all of us, all Palestinians, cannot go to Gaza, and Gazans cannot leave Gaza.

Gaza has a fascinating cuisine because of its proximity to Egypt and because after 1948 many people from coastal cities like Jaffa and Haifa ended up in Gaza for some time. So in the Gazan cuisine, you have this mix of beautiful dishes from all over Palestine. There's this dish that is made with aubergine, lentils, pomegranate juice, and tahini. It's a dish from Jaffa. It was preserved and still cooked in Gaza but totally forgotten in Jaffa. In this way the Gazan kitchen preserved those dishes, and people still cook them, though they add their own spices. They love, love, love, love dill seeds, and they add dill seeds to so many dishes that other cities don't. So there's this specificity. They keep creating new recipes because there's electricity cuts. They rely mostly on dishes that don't cost much money and can stay preserved outside the fridge. Or they recycle old recipes into new recipes that use ingredients you have today. It's an abundant kitchen, and it's really tasty. The way for me to research Gazan cuisine was to meet Gazans who left Gaza to live in the West Bank, but I use social media, too, to reach Palestinians all over the world.

Speaking of reaching people all over the world, your performance practice reaches only a handful of people at each performance. Could you talk about the table itself and why it has the form that it has? You could have a cooking show on TV, or you could be writing huge numbers of recipe books to transmit the cuisine all over the world, both to Palestinians living in other countries and to people who have no connection with the cuisine at all. Could you talk about why you chose performance?

I'm choosing this form for the time being. I love the form of the table. For me it's a way for us to reclaim this collectivity of eating together, of listening—which is really important for those performances. You are presented with a dish and you listen to the story. You

have the presence of people around you who you may or may not know. You have this artist sharing with you stories of the research, from a place you might have visited or you might have never visited. This moment of performance, when all those components come together, is a very specific thing that a cookbook cannot do. That doesn't mean that I might not make a cookbook later on: I might. But right now I feel I need to focus more on sharing in other ways. I give online classes, for instance. I cook all the time on Instagram, another way of sharing. But there's something magical about long tables with so many people who do not know each other—or who only know a few people around them—listening to these stories. It is a very specific form.

As you started to work with these tables as your structure, what surprised you? What did you discover about performance and working with the public that you perhaps didn't expect?

You always have stories after each performance because the people who attend them share things with you after, or even during, the performance that blow your mind. For me it's that excitement—a new experience—that makes me organize tables whenever I can. I started doing it in people's houses, and that was very special. Sometimes there were fifteen guests, sometimes twenty-five, and I learned a lot because I was a guest as well as a host. I was cooking with the hosting family, and it was not my story—the story of my research—but it was me highlighting the story of this family and the way it can help us understand Palestinianness in an expanding way. There was lots of intimacy in those first five events. The guests were invited; it was not an open call or open ticketing as I have done since. After that it kept growing, but it's always different. I always have to be attuned to who will show up at the table but at the same time to be open to whoever comes—to ensure that it will feel like a hospitable environment for whoever comes.

The first table happened in December 2017, and in 2018 there were many, many additional commissions in Palestine. After

Palestine Hosting Society's *Menu of Dis/Appearance.* Photo: Maria Baranova the autumn in 2019, it seemed like I would always do tables: I was working in Warsaw, in New York, and in Abu Dhabi. But then in between those events I would go to Palestine, do intense research for three weeks, and then proceed. 2020 was supposed to be a crazy busy year as well.

As you start to include ticket buyers in the tables, do you now think about the form as theater or performance or what? How is it an art practice beyond archiving, remembering?

Since the beginning, the project has been an extension of my art practice, and it was not made with the intention of archiving, of remembering, because I'm against the nostalgic form of remembrance. As an artist, I would never have that as part of my practice, and I was very critical of that in my work before Palestine Hosting Society. For me the value of this whole project is found in activating those recipes, those stories, bringing forth those people that I interview and I cook with, and collecting what is lost, what is left. I keep pushing it to new forms all the time. It has been live performances, but it might also become installations, videos, or all of those together. I just go with it. Maybe it will include other components—pottery pieces I construct for a special way of eating certain dishes, because pottery is also my practice as an artist. I think that the beauty of having a live art practice is that you don't rely on definitions of what's art or what's not art.

You said that when you're holding tables in Palestine, you always use Arabic—

Except in Jerusalem (*laughs*). There I do the performance in Arabic and English at the same time. So I say something in Arabic and then I translate it, but not in a boring way, in a way that's engaging for people who understand both languages at the same time.

Have Israelis come to the performances?

Yes, yes. I mean, not the Zionist Israelis but Israelis who want to celebrate the city. You don't speak Hebrew at my table, but as long as you respect the people around you and you listen, then you are welcome. We had beautiful, mixed audiences—foreigners, Palestinians, Israelis—and it was not a problem.

The subject of the performances is deeply political, and inherent in it is censorship and silencing. To use your word, it's about disappearance. Have you ever come across direct censorship or other pushback in your own practice?

So far, no. But when articles or videos about Palestine Hosting Society go viral, then you are open for everyone [to comment]. I remember when AJ+ made a video about Palestine Hosting Society, there were so many comments that came from people who just say, "What does she do exactly, food for a people that do not exist?" We are used to that as Palestinians; we are being questioned all the time: Do we exist? Does our land exist? Does our culture exist? It's part of the value of this whole project. In person, no, I was never opposed like that. In New York, as part of the festival, we had all kinds of people on the tables and people who had visited Palestine, people who had not, people who are Jewish, people who are Israeli—different, different people. But there was a sense of respect for the gift that is presented on the table. I think that's what food does. When there is food on the table, then people become more civilized, I think (*laughs*).

That's great! Is that inherent in the mission of your practice, to make people more civilized?

To listen and to have food creates an energy of listening and respect. It does not ask you to do anything—and sometimes that's all you need to listen to another person: to not be accused of something, to not be asked to do something, just to be in a space created for you to listen, to really listen to the stories of another.

And not only to listen with the ears but with all five senses at once.

Exactly. You're digesting the story; you're not only listening to it. You're really using all your senses to have this story become part of your being, and that's something really big, I think. That's why people come and talk after the performance, because they want to give back, they want to share their story or their relation to the place that you come from.

As you began to approach our invitation for you to create a table at Bard, what did you plan specifically for your first table in an American context?

I really wanted it to be about the story of the project, so I shared the research with people around one menu that highlights dishes and stories from different parts of Palestine. I didn't want to focus on one single practice, or one single city, or one single ingredient. I wanted it to be a journey, but this journey would be the project itself. I constructed the performance to focus on the people that I gathered those recipes from, to create this empathy in relation to the recipe, and the research, and the time during which I explored this recipe. It was like the whole thing was a story, and people can come in and out of it as they want, because I wanted them to enjoy the food and to focus on the food and to explore those tastes of the story and of the dish at the same time. We did lots of focus on locality as well. I wanted to know what ingredients were available at the venue, in upstate New York, so we wouldn't have to outsource so far away.

Could you tell me about a couple of the most special dishes that you included in the New York performances?

The carrots were very special on the menu—I remember the saga of the carrots. They were stuffed red carrots—not the orange ones but the red ones—and they are cooked in tamarind sauce. The carrots that we usually work with are the bigger ones, and they are easier to core. The corers that I had brought with me to the United States were confiscated at

the airport, so I didn't have my tools, and because those carrots were smaller, instead of having one carrot per person, we had to do two, so that meant it was a huge quantity of carrots that need to be cored. So we used carpenter's drills from the Fisher Center's scene shop—the carpenters did it all. Every step was a hassle because it was not being done in the kitchen; they had to go elsewhere to core them. And then the carrots we had were really

Palestine Hosting Society's *Menu of Dis/Appearance.* Photo: Maria Baranova

Palestine Hosting Society's *Menu of Dis/Appearance.* Photo: Maria Baranova

small—really, really thin. They were very delicious, and I was happy that they were on the menu, but I wouldn't put them on three performances one after the other (*laughs*). There was this other dish that I presented on the menu, the *maftoul*, which I had to roll by hand in a really traditional way. It's so hard even in Palestine to get fresh-made *maftoul*, but for me it was really one of the most important mains on this table, because I'd just learned the technique and the story of how to make this exact regional dish with those flavors before I went to New York. For me it was like bringing all those women and their skills with me to the table. So those are two of the dishes that were particular to the New York

events. The dessert was the Gazan *knafeh*, a pastry that was so much fun to put together, especially because I did it from scratch (*laughing*). But it was delicious and is easy to put together once you prepare the dough, and for me it was important to have Gaza very visible on the table. We had Gaza in two different dishes.

You also brought dishware with you from Palestine, ceramics and napkins. Could you tell me about the significance of that and why you do that in your practice?

I brought the wood molds as well that I pressed the yellow bread on, and it's a very specific design that reflects the connection of peasants with the earth in the design itself—in the visual of this print that the bread is pressed on. I usually travel with those wooden molds, but I also brought the pottery with me for the setup of the table and different objects. Because the whole menu was constructed in a way to tell the story of Palestine Hosting Society as a platform, it was important to have those previous tables somehow connected to this table, so we had some of the glass pieces from the Nablus table, and we printed the designs from the previous napkins on the other tables. They were characters in the narrative of the performance, and they needed to be visible. I brought some fresh ingredients as well with me, spices mostly. Especially some spices that are very specific to certain areas, like I bought the spice for the *kubbeh* from the best spice shop in Galilee, which everybody buys spices from—even the one who taught me, the master of *kubbeh* in that village. So, it was a way of creating those trails from Palestine to the table in New York through those flavors and objects and their stories.

In this moment, in the context of the global pandemic, maybe one of the most dangerous things we can do is to break bread together. Social distancing is the opposite of the structure of what you're creating when you bring people together. Are you thinking about tables or performances that actually could happen even if, let's say, the pandemic were to continue for another two years?

You're right, it's the exact opposite what I've done. I mean, for my research I need to meet people, I need to move. Now I cannot even do this. I cannot go to people's houses and just meet them and sit with them and cook with them, because of the fear of the virus, so it's not only the tables but the research as well

that's been affected. I hope it will not stay like this for another two years. I'm hopefully experimenting with video as one form of creating and of sharing this knowledge. So, somehow, I'm combining my practice before the Palestine Hosting Society with the food of Palestine Hosting Society to create videos, plus the writing and the interactive installations for shows that I'm working on. But I'm still hopeful that I'll be able to do tables again. If 2020 finished and we're still in this sphere, then maybe I need to think harder, but for me, I'm still hopeful. I'm cooking on Instagram, where I always add English descriptions. And one of the few good things about the pandemic is that you have time to cook.

Emilio Rojas's
*m(O)thers: Hudson
Valley*, LAB Biennial
*Where No Wall
Remains*, The
Fisher Center at
Bard, Annandale-
on-Hudson, NY,
2019. Photo: Maria
Baranova

Artist's Journal

Emilio Rojas

Naturalized Borders (an Open Wound in the Land, an Open Wound in the Body)

I came into the work of Gloria Anzaldúa (1942–2004) when one of my best friends, artist Guadalupe Martinez, gave me a copy of *Borderlands/La Frontera: The New Mestiza,* as a birthday gift eleven years ago. As she handed me the wrapped book, she said softly, "This book will change your life," and it did. Through her work, Anzaldúa has given me the words to understand my experience as a queer Latinx immigrant with indigenous heritage, battling identity and cultural hybridity while surviving and existing within multiple worlds. In my work I utilize my body in a political and critical way as an instrument to unearth removed traumas, embodied forms of decolonization, migration, and the poetics of space. It is essential to my practice to engage in the postcolonial ethical imperative to make visible and audible undervalued or disparaged sites of knowledge, narratives, and individuals. My research-based practice is heavily influenced by queer and feminist archives, border politics, botanical colonialism, and defaced monuments.

Anzaldúa wrote in *Borderlands,* "The us-Mexican border *es una herida abierta* (an open wound) where the Third World grates against the first and bleeds. . . . A borderland is a vague and undetermined place created by the emotional residue of an unnatural boundary. It is in constant state of transition."[1]

Two years ago I was invited to create a piece for *Where No Wall Remains* at Bard College, a four-day festival on the subject of borders—physical borders, political borders, and borders of the body—and how we might in time transcend them. This third edition of the LAB Biennial was cocurated by Lebanese artist Tania El Khoury and

Theater 51:1   DOI 10.1215/01610775-8824799

Emilio Rojas's *Naturalized Borders (to Gloria)*, LAB Biennial *Where No Wall Remains*, The Fisher Center at Bard, Annandale-on-Hudson, NY, 2019. Photo: Emilio Rojas

Gideon Lester, artistic director for theater and dance at Bard's Fisher Center. This invitation was extended to me through Ernesto Pujol, who recommended my practice to the curators. Pujol was a professor of mine in grad school at the School of the Art Institute of Chicago and knew about my work with migrants and refugees and the performances and pedagogy born from the archive of Gloria Anzaldúa. These series of works related to the border are all dedicated to Anzaldúa, who has inspired me to translate her archive, poetry, and theory into embodied gestures through collaborations with immigrant communities. Her work called me to respond through my body, through the land, and through the collective creation of a new border pedagogy that centers queer woman-of-color feminism—the Chicana feminism that Anzaldúa articulates. In this way every work from this series includes a parenthesis *(to Gloria)* inserted in the title to pay homage and delineate the lineage it follows and responds to. In the end I created three new works, which I will refer back to: *Naturalized Borders (to Gloria)*, *A Vague and Undetermined Place (to Gloria)*, and the continuing series *m(Other)s*.

I grew up visiting the border. My grandfather from my mother's side, Jose Manuel Balcázar Mendez, was a surgeon who ran a hospital in Tijuana, operating on Mexicans and Americans. My mother would have been born in San Diego, California, in 1947 right after WWII, but since ultrasound technology wasn't yet invented, the gender of the child couldn't be determined. My grandmother didn't want her children to be drafted to fight in the next American war (which she was sure would happen), in case they were born male. So she crossed the border to have her three children in Mexico, so my mom and her sisters would not be American.

The action that my grandmother took, crossing the border to have her children on the other side, is the opposite of the accusation that inspired the series *m(Other)s*. In the past few years, immigrant women have been accused of coming to the United States to birth their children, who are then derogatorily referred to by right-wing politicians as "anchor babies." *m(Other)s* is a series of video portraits of immigrant women, both documented and undocumented, holding their first-generation children, who are American by birthright under the protection of the Fourteenth Amendment. In a country that prides itself as a "nation of immigrants," these pieces serve as a reminder of the conditions of invisibility of immigrant women.

This work is inspired by the "hidden mother" photographs, common from the advent of photography up until the 1920s. I first found these images in an antique shop, and they were extremely haunting. I started collecting them because I was intrigued by the portraits of the infants in relation to these ghostly figures, disguised as chairs or camouflaged under fabric. Anzaldúa stated, "My job as an artist is to bear witness to what haunts us, to step back and attempt to see the pattern in the events (personal and societal) and how we can repair *el daño* (the damage) by using the imagination and its visions. I believe in the transformative power and medicine of art."[2] These photographs haunted me, and for a number of years they remained engrained in my memory as I kept collecting them. In the photographs the mothers are covered in order to hold their children in place for thirty seconds to a minute, until the photograph is exposed. Artist Laura Larson explained the process in her book *Hidden Mother*, "Photographing children presented the operator with a specific set of challenges. Pedestals and braces can't be used on the small, unruly bodies of infants. The photographer enlists the mother to play an instrumental role. Her body props the infant, steadying and comforting while the film is exposed."[3]

In the videos the m(other)s are covered by fabric with the stars of the American flag, creating a ghostly image that both references the historical photographs and protects their identity. The videos are in different tones of black and white and sepia and are slowed down so that the children move almost imperceptibly. These portraits seek to connect the political and social situation of women at the turn of the twentieth century with the invisibility of the labor and the rights of immigrant women today. I met the ten mothers who participated in the project through local community events, Latino organizations, and *La Voz*, a Spanish-language magazine that covered the project and used one of the portraits of the m(other)s as cover art.

The pieces serve as a dialectical image, as a moment from the past, a flash to the present, and a window into the future. These bilingual immigrant children are the future of our nation. Walter Benjamin stated in *The Arcades Project*, "It's not that what is past casts its light on what is present, or what is present its light on the past; rather, image is that wherein what has been comes together in a flash with the now to form a constellation."[4] These pieces form a constellation, which interpretation changes dramatically according to the political context; for example, when the government started separating children from their families, people who saw these videos thought the mothers were covered by the flag because the state held them captive. Currently with the discussion of removing birthright, the future of first-generation children of immigrants born in the United States has become uncertain. I have plans to continue doing the *m(Other)s* portraits in Pennsylvania, New York, Arizona, California, Texas, and across the United States, collaborating with different migrant organizations that are already supporting immigrant mothers locally. I will create more of these portraits for a survey exhibition of my work in relation to borders at Lafayette College in Pennsylvania, planned for the fall of 2021.

I remember the crossing of the border as a child, sitting on the back of the car in a hot summer, waiting for the lines of cars at the San Ysidro port of entry (one of the

Emilio Rojas's *m(O)thers: Hudson Valley*. Photo: Maria Baranova

fifty places where people can "legally" cross and the busiest land border crossing in the entire world). Vendors would approach the car; I would beg my mother to buy me a *paleta* (a Mexican icicle) to cool off—you could pay in pesos or dollars. I understood at a very early age that this was a point of inspection: we turned in our passports and visas to a man in a uniform; he asked questions and gave us permission to go through or not, or asked for a secondary inspection.

Little did I know at this point in my life that crossing borders and immigration inspections would become routine. The past thirteen years of living between Canada and the United States have made me extremely aware of my access and ability to move or not to move across borders. Being granted or denied student permits, working visas, permanent residency, green cards, Optional Practical Training, made me aware of my position as a Mexican immigrant who has been educated outside of my country of origin and how I perform and behave to be granted access. Poet Danez Smith asked in his book *Don't Call Us Dead*, "Do you know what is like to live on land who loves you back?"[5]

For the past seven years I've been developing new forms of border pedagogy, as a way to understand our collective and personal relationships to the US-Mexico border. How has the border been mediated and weaponized, and how does it act as a clear division "where the Third World grates against the first, and bleeds"?[6] This pedagogy attempts to continue the legacy of Chicana feminist writer, theorist, and educator Gloria Anzaldúa through the embodiment of her archives, hosted at the Benson Latin American Collection, University of Texas at Austin.

This open wound described by Anzaldúa and its relation to trauma as the emotional residue of a liminal geography have been at the core of what inspired me to teach and perform. Anzaldúa died in 2004 from complications of diabetes, but now more than ever her work is relevant to understand the tensions that continue to increase in this open wound where worlds grate against each other. This vague and undetermined place that bleeds through the lives of others is the emotional residue that clearly demarcates what is defined as the United States of America. Who is allowed in? Who is welcomed to stay?

In the opening poem to the book Anzaldúa wrote,

> 1950 mile-long open wound
> dividing a pueblo, a culture,
> running down the length of my body,
> staking fence roads in my flesh,
> splits me splits me
> me raja me raja,
> This is my home
> this thin edge of barbwire.
> But the skin of the earth is seamless.
> the sea cannot be fenced,
> el mar does not stop at borders.[7]

In the piece *Heridas Abiertas (to Gloria)*, translated as *Open Wounds (to Gloria)*, ongoing since 2014, a tattoo artist reopens every year the line of the US-Mexico border without ink in my back. The mark made from my first vertebra to my last creates a twenty-two-inch bleeding wound during the performance; then it becomes a scar, until it is reopened again. Rendering into the body the site where "the Third World grates against the first and bleeds,"[8] the skin becomes territory, the bleeding geography translated as a map and written in blood. During the performance, as the wound is made by the tattoo artist, the sound weaves the stories of immigrants who have crossed the border without documents, amplifying their experiences, and highlighting whatever they want to share about their crossing. The voices are anonymous and in Spanish, so only someone who understands the language is able to access these oral histories.

Rebecca Schneider wrote about this piece, "Having carved the borderline into his back as an inkless tattoo, he reopens the wound annually, reopening, recurring the line so that it moves like a long branch, bending and bleeding in tandem with his spine. . . . One time in another time, one's words into another's mouth, Rojas literalizes the ongoing, reopening lives and afterlives of historical trauma that move in spinal time among us, limb to limb, reaching for redress."[9]

After carving the border every year, I clearly feel the geography in the pain running down the length of my back. I also feel the wound heal every year as the open wound becomes as scar. In this way my body shows me, year after year, that healing is possible. Like the piece *Shibboleth* (2007) of artist Doris Salcedo, permanently inscribed in the floor of the Tate Modern, there is always a mark where trauma happened, a scar that is left as a reminder. I constantly ask myself, Could we truly heal the wounds the border has inflicted in the lives of so many of us?

I became obsessed with the formation of borders around the globe, the sociopolitical and historical implications of these lines forced into the land by wars, colonialism, imperialism, and the competition for resources, how borders have been used as sites where hatred and xenophobia are directed and mobilized toward immigrants and refugees. I began looking at the lines of borders, how when abstracted from the map they look like cracks or scars. I began finding them in walls and the pavement. Every fissure, crevice, and fracture became a border in my mind. I started drawing with pencil the actual geographical borders of Latin America on pieces of paper and continued following the lines until it became a sort of topography. These drawings are called *Topographies of the Margins*. They became a sort of meditation, as I drew hundreds upon hundreds of lines, thinking about the liminal spaces in between and what each line represented and separated. Who drew the borders as we know them today?

After visiting Bard for the first time, I returned to Mexico to visit my family. On a plane on the way back I was doing one of these drawings of the borders, and as I looked down from the plane I saw a field of corn that was following the outline of a river. The corn wasn't planted on straight rows, instead it followed the contours of the landscape, and I imagined the border being planted as a line of corn in a field, and the idea of the piece *Naturalized Borders (to Gloria)* began.

Emilio Rojas's
*Naturalized Borders
(to Gloria)*. Photo:
Emilio Rojas

Anzaldúa compares the mestiza, the mix-raced woman of indigenous and European ancestry, to corn: "Indigenous like corn, the mestiza is a product of crossbreeding, designed for preservation under a variety of conditions. Like an ear of corn—a female seed-bearing organ—the mestiza is tenacious, tightly wrapped in the husks of her culture. Like kernels she clings to the cob; with thick stalks and strong brace roots, she holds tight to the earth—she will survive the crossroads."[10] For Mexicans, corn is not just a crop but a deep cultural symbol connected to our diet, daily life, ancestry, and traditions. According to Aztec cosmology, the first humans were shaped out the dough of maize—we are the people of the corn. Originally corn was domesticated from a grass called teosinte by peoples of Mesoamerica about 10,000 years ago, in what is now the southwest of Mexico. Corn that now grows across the globe is often referred to as the greatest agronomic achievement. It occupies one-fourth of all cultivated land in the United States, over 90 million acres, and is the second largest crop in the world after sugar cane in Brazil.

Naturalized Borders (to Gloria) was a land art and community-based project, including an eighty-foot-long line of indigenous crops. This installation is in the shape of the US-Mexico border and is planted with corn, squash, beans (the three sisters), and teosinte. The gatekeeper of the garden is the teosinte, the ancestor of what we know as corn today. Bard College and the farm are located on the ancestral homelands of the Muhheaconneok or Mohican people, known today as the Stockbridge-Munsee Mohican Nation. The eight-month-long project, which began in March 2019, when the crops were planted from seed, was developed in collaboration with Rebecca Yoshino (manager of the farm) and the Center for the Study of Land, Air, and Water, with the participation of students Mary Elizabeth Klein, Meghan Mercier, Kaitlyn McClelland, Gabrielle Reyes, Alexi Piirimae, Midori Barandiaran, and Austin Sumlin.

The installation grew through the summer, and when students came back to school I organized workshops, exercises, and community events to reimagine and embody our own relationship to the border. Continuing the legacy of Anzaldúa, the work attempted to unearth histories of immigration, labor rights, borders, land sovereignty, and systemic oppression.

The three sisters configuration of corn, squash, and beans, is a traditional method used by indigenous communities in Central and North America, where the crops work

Emilio Rojas's
*Naturalized Borders
(to Gloria)*. Photo:
Emilio Rojas

together in a symbiotic relationship. The beans fix nitrogen into the soil that feeds the corn, while the corn provides poles for the beans to grow up but also is anchored by the root system of the beans. The large, prickly, and kidney-bean-shaped leaves of the squash prevent weeds from growing, regulate soil temperature/moisture, and provide a pest barrier. The three sisters remind us of our interdependence with our environment, and when eaten together they provide a complete plant-based nutritional diet.

The piece also served as homage to Gloria Anzaldúa, whose family had worked in the agricultural fields of Texas for generations. She herself paid for her undergraduate degree working in the fields. Her family was dispossessed of their lands when Texas became independent and then part of the United States after the treaty of Guadalupe Hidalgo on February 2, 1848. The treaty "left 100,000 Mexican citizens on this side, annexed by conquest along with the land."[11] Today about forty indigenous tribes straddle the border; the line cuts through their territories, as well as disrupting the migration patterns of thousands of species. This reminds me of the rallying cry of the Mexican/Chicanx immigrant rights movement: "We didn't cross the border, the border crossed us."

The work developed as a series of encounters, with the land, the archive, the more than four hundred students who attended the workshops, my students in class, and members of the community. Through the visits of students, I developed different exercises to think about our relationship with the border. They involved movement, critical texts, writing, poetry, drawings, discussions, soundscapes, performances, harvesting, and the sharing of food.

One of the written exercises was to imagine if you had the chance to sit with the border at a table for dinner: what questions would you ask her/him/them, and who would you be addressing? The collection of questions straddle poetics and politics, a job interview and a first date. Some participants took the questions very seriously, while others tried to use humor to deflect the tension of the subject and the violence that this site brings to mind. My attempt now is to transcribe the hundreds of questions and publish a small book with them. Here are some examples of the questions the participants wrote:

Have you lost count of how many people have passed through you? Or died trying?
Which side of the bed do you sleep in, the Mexican Side or the American Side?
Do you call the Canadian-us border and bitch about the us politics?
Are you a highly functional introvert or a sensory extrovert?
Do you speak to your children in English, Español, Spanglish?
Did your mother ever warn you about to talking to strangers?
How do you sleep at night with the horrors you have seen?
When you were established, was it against your own will?
What is your favorite and least favorite part of yourself?
Who would you choose to write your auto-biography?
Do you go to group therapy with other borders?
What is your favorite bird that flies above you?
Have you ever been separated from your family?
Do you hold their hands as they die in your deserts?
Do you have an Instagram? How many followers?
What is your shoe size? Do you like wearing hills?
When was the last time you cried? You laughed?
Do you hear the children crying at night in cages?
Do you have blood stains in the clothes you wear?
Do you count monarch butterflies to fall asleep?
Have you ever prepared for the apocalypse?
What skeletons do you keep in your closet?
Have you held the hand of a dying lover?
What language do you dream in?
Where do your thoughts wander?
What type of car do you drive?
Do you ever blame yourself?
Where is the greener grass?
What is your biggest fear?
Would you marry a Mexican?
What is the color of your skin?
Do you have trust issues?

Are you always just vigilant?

Do you sometimes look the other way?

Have you ever thought about moving somewhere else?

Do you think it's possible one day for you to disappear?

Do you know how to swim across your own rivers?

Do you wish you could take your symbolism back?

Do you pay your taxes late every year?

Are you more of a night owl, an early raiser?

What are some words you would use to describe yourself?

Who are your friends and who are your enemies?

Do you sometimes look the other way?

How does the breeze feel in your skin?

Do you believe in the American Dream?

How many languages do you speak?

Would you rather be a wall or a bridge?

Have you ever been in an abusive relationship?

What is your relationship to your parents like?

How far north have you ever traveled?

Cuales son tus rutinas de la mañana?

Where do you find your strength?

What makes you feel at home?

What are your daily rituals?

Who do you protect?

Do you love yourself?

Will they return?

As migrants crossing borders, we are always asked questions by immigration officers: Where are you coming from? Do you know everything that is in that bag? Have you ever entered the United States "illegally?" How long are you planning to stay in this country? I have collected the questions since I moved to Canada and then later the United States, alongside all the questions I got asked for every visa or green card I've had to apply for. The underlying assumption is that you are lying, and many times the same questions get asked in different configurations to see if you answer differently or if you falter. As migrants we are used to being interrogated, questioned, and having to prove ourselves with our answers. We are not used to asking questions back, especially of those in power. As the border becomes anthropomorphized in the exercise, it reverses that position. After participants write the questions, I go through a series of exercises of using their voice and how they can read a question: whisper it, shout it, share it. The part of the corn where the kernels grow tightly wrapped in a husk is called an ear, so after sharing their questions with one another they dispersed in the installation and found an

ear to whisper the questions they had to the border. The corn is planted in the shape of the line of the border, so the questions go back into the border and remain unanswered, but perhaps heard—to whisper in an ear, so the land might listen. An intimate as well as poetic gesture, to whisper into someone's ear is a close and confidential exchange where no one else can listen to what has been uttered. For me a question works as a seed. It might not bloom immediately, it might be dormant for years, it might need fire like the seed of a sequoia for it to sprout, but once it's uttered there is the potential for it to grow.

Will the land respond back to us? This question makes me think of Anishinaabe artist Rebecca Belmore's piece *Ayum-ee-aawach Oomama-mowan: Speaking to Their Mother* (1991, 1992, 1996). For this work, Belmore built a six-foot-wide, seven-foot-long extension to a megaphone, and with the conical sculpture she amplified the sound to speak to the land. The piece was meant to respond to the Oka Crisis of 1990, but it then traveled across Canada and the United States, addressing the land from coast to coast. Belmore wrote about this work,

Emilio Rojas's *Naturalized Borders (to Gloria)*. Photo: Emilio Rojas

73

> This artwork was my response to what is now referred to in Canadian history as the "Oka Crisis." During the summer of 1990, many protests were mounted in support of the Mohawk Nation of Kanesatake in their struggle to maintain their territory. This object was taken into many First Nations communities—reservation, rural, and urban. I was particularly interested in locating the Aboriginal voice on the land. Asking people to address the land directly was an attempt to hear political protest as poetic action.[12]

Perhaps the land responds back to us, in a language we do not understand, and if we did, are we ready to listen? Maybe the harvest of the three sisters offered some answers, or the questions that were whispered in the ears of the corn were answered or talked about in the conversations that happened during the decolonial feast we prepared with the corn, squash, and beans. As part of the installation we also invited Sean Sherman, Oglala Lakota from the Pine Ridge reservation and founder of the Sioux Chef, who spoke about the r(e)volition of indigenous food systems in North America, linking land sovereignty to how we prepare and grow our food. If we are what we eat, we can decolonize our bodies by decolonizing our diet.

This exercise occurred to me after reading Pablo Neruda's *El libro de las preguntas* (*Book of Questions*), finished months before his death in September 1973, and after reading the book *Tell Me How It Ends: An Essay in Forty Questions* by fellow Bard faculty writer Valeria Luiselli. Neruda's *El libro de las preguntas* is composed entirely of unanswerable couplets and was his last poem, in which he juxtaposes the maturity of his late work and the imagination of a child. Neruda questioned with poetic mastery what lies beyond our ability to name. Similarly, in Luiselli's text there are no answers, only questions that are drawn from the questionnaire created by immigration attorneys for the thousands of undocumented children from Central America who have arrived at the US-Mexico border since 2014. Many of the questions on issues surrounding the border remain unanswered, and perhaps the only way to go deeper is to constantly ask more questions. One of the questions Neruda asks in *El libro de las preguntas* is "¿Porque enseña el professor / La geografia de la muerte?"[13] The question translates to "Why does the professor teach the geography of death?" I stand in front of Jason De León's installation *Hostile Terrain 94*, a twenty-foot-long map of the Arizona-Mexico border with 3,117 handwritten toe tags, which provide information about "those who have died while migrating, including name (if known), age, sex, cause of death, condition of body, and location."[14] I cannot help but to think about this geography of death, the site where so many bodies in decomposition were found, the wound that keeps spilling the blood of so many migrants hoping for a better future. Why do I teach about the border, and why have I been so invested in creating new border pedagogies? Perhaps because this site is taught to us only as a geography of death and not as a rich and valuable space of transition, resilience, survival, and transformation, what Anzaldúa describes as "the

Emilio Rojas's *Naturalized Borders (to Gloria)*. Photo: Emilio Rojas lifeblood of two worlds merging to form a third country, a border culture."[15] Is it possible to see the border with different eyes than the lens the media and politicians have cast on it? For me some of these answers lie hidden in Anzaldúa's archive, and my work has been to dig them out and breathe into them new life, disperse her seeds and questions into the world.

The word for a piece of paper in Spanish is *hoja*, which is the same word for a leaf of a plant, crop, or a tree. So in another exercise in the installation I inserted the scanned texts and images of the archive into the corn in the field. In this way the archive was harvested from the corn itself, and students would walk through the maze of the corn and find the pieces of the archive, read them out loud, and then put them back so other people would find them. The work also developed with initiatives from the students. For example, one day as we were harvesting the archive, a student holding a copy of Anzaldúa's birth certificate told the group her birthday was coming up on September 26, exactly a week from that day. Although Anzaldúa died from complications of diabetes in 2004, at age sixty-one, we celebrated her seventy-seventh birthday with food and readings of her poetry and unpublished writings. The student herself baked a corn cake, and we had a gathering with tamales and music.

Another exercise was to draw the border from memory on a blank piece of paper, without seeing a map or any geographical reference. The instructions were: "Draw from memory the line that represents the border from one edge of the paper to another, try to be as accurate as possible and think about the territories you are cutting through as you draw the line if the left edge of the paper was the Pacific Ocean and the Right edge of the paper was the Atlantic." (If you have some time, please grab a piece of paper and follow these instructions yourself.) Each line drawn was completely different from the other, since no one really knows what the line of the border looks like. As Anzaldúa stated, "A borderland is a vague and undetermined place created by the emotional residue of an unnatural boundary."[16] How is it that the site that defines so much of our identity, nationalism, and "belonging" can be so abstract and blurry when it comes to knowing its shape or what it traverses? How do we not know the ways in which the border changes the migration patterns of flora and fauna or how it cuts through indigenous territories? This exercise reminded me of the time when in the height of the Iraq war a reporter went around major US cities with a world globe (with borders but no names of countries) and asked Americans to point to the where Iraq was located in the globe: almost no one could.

This exercise with the students led to the last piece I created for the LAB Biennial, titled *A Vague and Undetermined Place (to Gloria)*. This piece is a mobile *paleta* cart-turned-drawing studio on which participants are invited to draw the line of the southern border in exchange for a *paleta* (Mexican popsicle) that I made with Mexican produce from across the border (mangos, avocados, prickly pear, guavas). As with much of my work, it developed slowly and organically, giving time for questions to germinate and grow, as well as for relations to be developed and not forced. I work on multiple projects simultaneously, in what I like to describe as steady-paced multitasking. When working

Emilio Rojas's
*Naturalized Borders
(to Gloria)*. Photo:
Emilio Rojas

with communities I find this mode of working to be more ethical: it allows for time for trust to be built, for friendship to be developed with collaborations, and for a true and long-lasting engagement with the communities that I work with that goes beyond the initial timeline of any project. I was planning to continue this piece in community events and public spaces throughout this summer, exchanging *paletas* for drawings of the line of the border, which is in the end only a vehicle to facilitate conversations around the subject of immigration, borders, and displacement, but the pandemic made this extremely difficult to realize. I would also like to publish the exercises drawn from the workshops created during the *Naturalized Borders (to Gloria)* and from my experiences working with migrant and refugee youth. This will be a practical tool for educators to use with their students to understand and think through the border from an embodied experience.

In the end, for the final performance of *Naturalized Borders (to Gloria)*, once the crops were harvested and the stalks completely dried, we returned the land to its original state by unplanting the installation, metaphorically taking down the border and burning it in a communal fire. Many of the students who participated in the workshops and who worked on the piece participated in this performance. Because we weren't allowed to burn the installation in the open field, we took the stalks into a fire pit at the center of campus, a procession that migrated the border before its destruction. The labor of taking out the stalks, cutting the roots, and creating the bundles to carry took many hours, and in the end there was a sense of completion and cathartic release from the performance for a piece that had taken eight months of labor, growing, harvesting, workshops, dinners, conversations, and exchange.

I want to finish with an unpublished text I found in Anzaldúa's archive called "Citizen Earth." This passage was written by typewriter and corrected by hand. When I read it, I felt like she was talking directly to me, specifically in the part in which your roots can also become your prison—you can become trapped in the territory of your identities. In the end she calls for the complete abolition of borders and nationalism, which she believes is the solution to many of the world's problems:

> Yes, I acknowledge the deep silences that surge up from my Indian soul, the song that gives wing to my Spanish and the culture of the queer and the alien hidden somewhere in the deep recesses of my body, all these are my roots. My being influenced by the Anglo culture and schools I attended. All these are my roots but I would like them to not become my prison. I would like not to be trapped in the territory labeled woman mexican lesbian poet visionary. Nationalism, and borders have decimated and have come close to exterminating the human tribe. At the risk of sounding simplistic I believe that the issue of sexuality, of world hunger, and world war stem from the same problem and has the same solution, to stop plugging up the holes on our walls, to stop protecting our borders and territories, to stop making others "different" from ourselves and therefore "alien" and therefore "enemy" (from "Del toro Lado" a poem in progress).[17]

Notes

1. Gloria Anzaldúa, *Borderlands/La Frontera: The New Mestiza* (San Francisco: Aunt Lute, 1999), 25.

2. Gloria Evangelina Anzaldúa Papers, Box 32, Folder 2, Benson Latin American Collection, University of Texas at Austin.

3. Laura Larson, *Hidden Mother* (Baltimore: Saint Lucy, 2016), 8.

4. Walter Benjamin, *The Arcades Project*, ed. Rolf Tiedemann, trans. Howard Eiland and Kevin McLaughlin, 4th printing (Cambridge, MA: Harvard University Press, 2003), 462nn2–3.

5. Danez Smith, *Don't Call Us Dead: Poems* (Minneapolis: Graywolf, 2017), 8.

6. Anzaldúa, *Borderlands/La Frontera*, 25.

7. Ibid., 24.

8. Ibid., 25.

9. Rebecca Schneider, "Taking Instructions for Becoming," in *The Methuen Drama Companion to Performance Art*, ed. Bertie Ferdman and Jovana Stokic (London: Bloomsbury, 2020), 83.

10. Anzaldúa, *Borderlands/La Frontera*, 103.

11. Ibid., 29.

12. Rebecca Belmore, *"Ayum-ee-aawach Oomama-mowan: Speaking to Their Mother,"* www.rebeccabelmore.com/exhibit/Speaking-to-Their-Mother.html (accessed September 21, 2020).

13. Pablo Neruda, *The Book of Questions*, trans. William O'Daly, 2nd ed. (Port Townsend, WA: Copper Canyon, 2001), 7.

14. Live Arts Bard, "Live Arts Bard Presents Jason De León: *Hostile Terrain 94 (HT94),"* fishercenter.bard.edu/events/ht94/ (accessed September 21, 2020).

15. Anzaldúa, *Borderlands/La Frontera*, 25.

16. Ibid.

17. Gloria Anzaldúa, "Citizen Earth," Anzaldúa Papers, Box 55, Folder 2.

Rudi Goblen's *Fito*,
LAB Biennial *Where
No Wall Remains*,
The Fisher Center
at Bard, Annandale-
on-Hudson, NY, 2019.
Directed by Michael
Yawney. Lighting
design by Elayne
Bryan. Featuring
musicians Andrews
"Nonms" Mujica
and Daniel "Felix"
Garcia. Photo: Maria
Baranova

Rudi Goblen

Fito

A Concert Play

Author's Note

In 1979, during the uprising of the Sandinista revolution, many middle-class and wealthy families fled Nicaragua, initiating a wave of Nicaraguan refugees into the United States, the largest wave of documented immigrants at the time. Although the initial overthrow of the Somoza regime was a bloody affair, the u.s.-funded Contra War that followed took the lives of tens of thousands of Nicaraguans. The caravan of depleted Nicaraguan immigrants, of all classes, did not end until 1989.

    Most of those Nicaraguan immigrants during that period were women: there were only sixty male Nicaraguan immigrants for every one hundred female immigrants. My mother was one among the mass of many to migrate, bringing my older brother and me along with dreams in her chest and hopes in her hands of giving us a worthier life.

    Today, 350,000 Nicaraguans reside in the United States; almost 50 percent of them live in Miami, and 25 percent of them where I grew up, Sweetwater, Florida, also known as "Little Managua." My connection to this play starts here, this is us—a people who fled their homeland to escape war and political and economic torment, a noble people, practical people.

    But what happens when those who fled to escape can settle only in the poor and deteriorated sections of their newfound country, a place where your skin color and accent define your class?

    What happens when racial discrimination not only surrounds you but breeds among your own people?

Production Note

This piece is performed in the round and works best inside intimate/alternative performance spaces. The circle it is performed in is not a holy space or a barricade—it is just a circle. There's a lot of music in this piece; people will feel impelled to move to it and might scratch the itch to go into that circle. As a matter of fact, you can encourage them to do so—without saying so, of course. Embrace that, and adjust accordingly to the impulses of the audience.

    no chairs. The audience will be standing/sitting around the circle and the rest of the space. Absolutely no curtain speeches or prerecorded welcomes at the top of the show either—none.

    us (the pronoun) is a character in the play. u.s. (the acronym) is said throughout the text of the play.

    Please differentiate the two.

Theater 51:1   doi 10.1215/01610775-8824813

SCRIPT NOTES

[*beat*] = a quick breath.

[*rest*] = a longer breath.

italicized text = emphasis on a word.

[*silence*] = a moment to think/let things settle.

[*pf*] = the pronunciation of the sound made
by a kick drum.

beats, *rests*, and *silences* should all be treated
as musical notations to honor the pace of the
language.

PEOPLE

FITO (*pronounced in Spanish*)
latinx man

DRUMMER/BASS GUITARIST
latinx man

PERCUSSIONIST
latinx man

US
played by FITO

ANDROID
played by musician

PLACE

an outline of a circle made with white chalk,
sand, and/or white tape.

instruments are placed at the upstage edge of
the circle.

TIME

now.

THE OFFICE

bright lights bump on,

*mostly focusing on the microphone placed upstage
of the circle.*

VOICE-OVER
Hello everyone!
My name is Brad Stevens,
I'm the immigration
services assistant here.
I'm going to start off today's ceremony.
When I'm done here
I'm gonna turn it over to
Miss Laura Pierce here.
She is a bill officer,
and *she* will be administrating you.

There's a couple of things that we'd like to go
      over first.
One, we're asked all the time,
can you take photographs
or videos of today's ceremony?

Absolutely!
This is your ceremony.
Feel free to take all the pictures
and video that you want.
All we're asking—well—
that, if you have a cell phone,
please put them all on silent right now.
We've had some very *strange* ringtones
in the past, *we don't want them today.*
Alright?

After the ceremony's over,
I will open these doors.
These will be the doors you go out.

Also if you wanna stay after
and take some photographs of the room
while you're at the ceremony,
feel free to do so.
All we ask is the stage area—
we're working on a couple of things here,
please keep off the stage,
we don't wanna have any issues today.

So, but, you can take all the pictures you
          want,
in the rest of the room.
What we'd like to do
before we start,
is we like to start off
with the national anthem.
We have a flag over here.
So can I have everyone please stand?
If you have a hat,
please remove it at this time.

bump to black

THE INTRO

music track plays.

*in the dark, we hear heavy, thick, meditative
baselines and singing bowls. indigenous chants
and drumming far off in the distance. lights
slowly fade up to a dim setting to find three
silhouettes standing on the outskirts of the circle,
maybe even within the audience.*

*they're all in suits, in a trance of sorts, walking
slowly toward the center. one is carrying a clave,
one a shaker, the other a tambourine.*

*they mouth various chants as they move forward.
once they reach the instruments, they stop
chanting and walking.*

*the music keeps going. the drummer sits and starts
playing along first. next the percussionist walks
to his instruments and starts to play along. lastly,
FITO walks to the microphone at the rise of the
song.*

lights shift.

*note: this section should feel like a light show. a
concert. aggressive. red. moving lights. flashing
lights. violent light, warm light. gobos.*

the three men begin playing fast-paced rhythms

*and vigorously moving their bodies. releasing
something, shaking something out. this continues
for the rest of the song.*

lights and music come to a complete stop.

THE WELCOME

*sounds of static, shortwave radios and a robot/
machine breaking down are heard.*

FITO is startled. he looks around baffled.

*he sees a half man/half machine behind him,
walking toward him. FITO is edged out of the
circle as ANDROID gets closer and closer.*

*a robotic dance solo by ANDROID, interpreting
what is being said, takes place.*

ANDROID (robotic voice-over)
Welcome to
U.S.
You are here you are here.
Con
grats.
You are here
you are wel
comed.
You are.
Please,
before you.
No be
fore you.
Enter.
Wipe your mouth.

Dust
your pride off.
We will need that.

We will
we will,
we.
We need
no want

we want you
to need us.

Us is us is.
It is in our name us.
U.S.

The United States of being united are in a bad
    state.
Various states.
De
nial.
De
lusion.
Wo
rry
and
anx
I, I, I.

I am
sorry that is my opinion.
Please leave all opinions here.
Before you enter.
There is no need for that.

We will provide you the opinion you need.
We will provide you the info you need.
We we.
We will provide for you,
for you
and your new family is us for you.
We are here.
You are here.
Welcome.
What is your blood type?
Do you love us?
Are you here alone?
Take this gun, you will need it.
Take this drug, you will need it.
Take this god,
just take.
Just take.
Just.
Take this.

Take this take.
We will.
We will take what we want.
Are you here to be taken?
Welcome.
You have notifications.
You have new messages you.
You just got a ticket.
Please pay
your ticket.
You must pay
your ticket.
Your ticket is overdue over you.
You are over, this is
almost over, this is.
Thank you for paying!
You are great!
Like your country again.
Make America your country.
Step over that line and
that line you cross will be your boundary.
Do not do not.
Cross that line
during your visit.
Stay between the lines.
In order the order of new, we like order.
Your order is here.
Did you order?
We have online, car rides, food, wives, drugs
    and sex you can order.
Just
stay in,
do not get
out of
line, do not.
Do not go out,
stay in,
in.
In order
you will stay.
Stay out of the way.
Welcome. Welcome.
Take this.

Take it.
And
keep going
before we.
We.
We change our mind often.
Be ready.
Be
well.
Be sick.
Be
free.
Be dumb be.
Freedom.
Be quiet.
Be quiet.
Be quiet
Shut the trump up.
Shhhhh.
Come in.
Welcome.

ANDROID *exits downstage of the circle.*

THE MONSTER

lights bump up on the stage left edge of the circle.

we see US.

US
Hii!! I'm US,
and I like to build monsters.
And I've been doing it for a pretty long time.
You can sorta say it's like my favorite thing
        to do
in the whole wide . . . uh . . . room. . . . yea!

Now, I'm sure you're probably asking yourself,
"Do monsters even exist?" Yes! They do.

And I'm pretty sure you're also asking
        yourself,
"Well then, how do I build a monster?"

And that's exactly what brought you here
        today.
So! Let's just get into it.

Now, there's a couple of things you're going to
        need to know
about building a monster even before we even
        get started.
For instance, you're gonna need a whole lotta
        space.
High ceilings are a plus, so if you live in a
        mansion, thumbs up.

Two,
if you're over eighteen years old watching this
        tutorial right now,
GET OUT OF HERE!!!
No one wants to deal with your *adult brain.*
We're fucking creating here.

Three,
make sure you're home alone.
You don't wanna scare the monster off once
        you're done.

Four.
You're gonna fail.

[*rest*]

Yea, you're gonna fail.

[*beat*]

Over and over again.
Every last single one of you is going to
        fail—miserably.
You probably won't even make it halfway
        through.
'Cause you never finish anything you get
        started anyhow.
Why? Because you're lazy. So do yourself a
        favor,
no, you know what, do me a favor, stop
        wasting my time,
and turn off this video off right now!

US *freezes and waits for the audience to leave. his eyeballs should be the only thing moving here.*

this takes as long as it needs to take.

[*silence*]

Five!
If you're still here, you passed the test!
And you showed dedication, appreciation,
    and motivation.
Good work!

Speaking of work. I hope you have a pen and
    paper ready.
Let's talk ingredients!

Candy!
A whole lot of candy.
A pound of haloes.
A pound of horns.
A witch's tongue.
A side of sin.
A dash of cinnamon.
Salt, sugar, milk.
Organic eggs.
Sunflowers.
The devils tail.
God's hair . . . and *blood.*

[*rest*]

Any kind . . .

[*rest*]

I don't care where you get it from.

[*beat*]

Drugs—the good kind!
And the *three* most important ingredients
    you're gonna need.
A huge garbage bag, an old mirror, and a
    large cup of coffee.

Now, take that old mirror
and place it on the ground right in front of
    you.

Now, I want you to take all the ingredients on
    our list
and throw them into that garbage bag—
make sure everything fits nice and
    comfortable.

Now, stand right over it and say, "Fuck you!"
    . . . "I love you,"
Now, tie a double knot on the garbage bag
    and make sure it's nice and tight.
Now, just to make sure nothing is going to
    get out,
I want everyone to pick up their garbage bags,
and all together, at the same time,
we are going to swing it around nice and slow
    about three times—
and again—we'll do this *all together*, like a
    nice ensemble.

Here we go.

Onnnnne . . .

Twooooooo,

Three—hold it right there. I want you to
    know something.
When we place this garbage bag on the
    ground
there is going to be a blackout. So we're gonna
    place them down on the floor,
all together, at the same time, on the count of
    . . . one . . . . . two . . . . and . . . . .
    . . . three.

bump to black

*improvised drumming, percussion, scatting, and
beatboxing happen in the dark.*

lights bump back on.

Now, I want you to take that garbage bag and
    move it to the side.
Bend down and carefully grab the old mirror
    we placed on the floor earlier.

Slowly pick it up, taking one hand and placing
    it right under the other,
and *slowly* bring it up to your face.

Because, if you followed all directions
    correctly,
you will slowly start to see . . .

your very own,
brand new
personal

monster.

[*beat*]

Now let's go get that cup of coffee.

bump to black

FITO *turns upstage and quickly walks toward the
microphone in the dark.*

The Poem

*note: the HAHs and FUCK in brackets during this
spoken-word piece are not only said by* FITO
*but are also accompanied by the bass, kick, snare
drum, and lights as well.*

lights bump on.

FITO
Hit me!
[*HAH! HAH! HAH!*]
My life's poem is a covered up tattoo
living on this God's neck
screaming out "fuck you, I'm alive
as much as you don't think I am!"
[*HAH! HAH! HAH!*]
A thick warrior-hand
planting its text on your DNA's chest
cracking its ass-phalt.
[*HAH! HAH! HAH!*]

Rudi Goblen's
Fito. Photo: Maria
Baranova

Be-longing, othering, them-ing,
they-ing, us-ing. All. The. Time.
I mean, why wouldn't the ones
spearing the spiraling-dark concur
that her and him only mean *me*,
equaling *you*, and *you*,
sir, ma'am, will never understand
what it takes to be a man
[*HAH!*]
comma
[*HAH!*]
when you're a single woman
raising two of her opposites
who have run amok on the streets
'cause they know no better.
[*HAH!*]
Ahhhhh.
[*HAH!*]
My mother.
[*HAH!*]
Ahhhhh.
[*HAH!*]
I love her.

[*beat*]

And put no one else above her.

[*beat*]

See, I was raised by two,
mama and gran,
with no macho in sight.
So yes, I cross my legs when I sit.

[*beat*]

And this ain't got shit to do with shit,
but I even sit when I pee.
What?
You don't?
Not even when you're tired?
Or sleepy?

[*beat*]

Man, get the fuck outta here . . .

deep inhale

Yes, I wear essential oils on my temples
instead of pumping big-pharma bullshit
        inside my body.
I gives no fucks about the talk-uh-tits and
        sports,
and obviously, I'm into the arts.
I'm also into cooking. Matter fact.
This morning,
I made a pan-roasted-almond-crusted-extra-
        firm-tofu-curry-sitting-on-top-a-bed-
        uh-greens
with a flaxseed-oil and lemon-vinaigrette
and it was vegan-gluten-free as *shhhhhh*.

[*beat*]

Understand this,
I don't like to curse in my pieces.
Ehhhhh, not too much,
but sometimes
you just got to add a [*FUCK*]
at the end of a sentence.
You feel me?

[*HAH!*]
Ahhhhh.
[*HAH!*]
My mother.
[*HAH!*]
Ahhhhh.
[*HAH!*]
I love her.

MILE 187

live music/rapping here.

Hah! It's just a regular night,
driving down the street not a jacker in sight.

Hah! I got calm too quick,
I stopped at the light, saw a cop, oh shit.

Uh! Play it cool my meng,
everything's still chill till the cop changes
        lanes.

Uh! There he go, there he go,
he turned on the sirens messing with my flow.

Fuck! Now I gotta pull on over,
slowed down the car, I stopped at the
shoulder.

Man. Here he come, here he come,
knocking on my window with his
muthafuckin' gun,

like "HOLD! FREEZE! GET THE FUCK OUT!
HANDS IN THE AIR I WILL SHOOT YA ASS
NOW!

WHAT?! GET ON YOUR KNEES NOW, SON!"
I don't want to die so I started to run.

I'M RUNNIN'
HA. YEA YEA
×4

This all just a dream.

I'M RUNNIN'
HA. YEA YEA
×4

This all just a dream.
This all just a dream.
This all just a dream.
This all just.
An American dream.

This all just.
This all just.
This all *justice*.
It's just us.

Hah! It's just a regular night,
driving down the street not a jacker in
sight.

Hah! I got to calm too quick,
I stopped at the light, saw a cop, oh shit.

Uh! Play it cool my meng,
everything's still chill till the cop
changes lanes.

Uh! There he go, there he go,
he turned on the sirens messing with my flow.

Fuck! Now I gotta pull on over,
slowed down the car, I stopped at the
shoulder.

Man. Here he come, here he come,
knocking on my window with his
muthafuckin' gun,

Rudi Goblen's
Fito. Photo: Maria
Baranova

"HOLD! FREEZE! GET THE FUCK OUT!
HANDS IN THE AIR I WILL SHOOT YA ASS
      NOW!

WHAT?! SON! GET ON YOUR KNEES!"
I don't want to die so I did what he need.

an interlude

FITO *improvises explaining where he was going
to an officer pointing a gun at him.*

he is handcuffed and forced to his knees.

*with his back to the audience, he rocks out for the
rest of the break in the song.*

*before the interlude is over, he breaks free from
the handcuffs, stands up, and repeats the hook one
last time.*

I'M RUNNIN'
HA. YEA YEA
×4

This all just a dream.

I'M RUNNIN'
HA. YEA YEA
×4

This all just a dream.

This all just a dream.

This all just a dream.

This all just.
An American dream.

This all just.
This all just.
This all *justice.*
It's just us.

NIGHTFALL

note: FITO *picks up the tambourine and plays it
in this song.*

live music and rapping here.

Freeduummb. *×3*

I. Want. To. Be. Free. Like. You

Freeduummb. *×3*

I. Want. To. Be. Free. Like. You

guitar solo

Freeduummb. *×3*

I. Want. To. Be. Free. Like. You

Freeduummb. *×3*

I. Want. To. Be. Free. Like. You

YOU!
The man at the top
The man who makes rules
The man with the power
YOU!
The man with the loot
The man who makes money
The man of the hour
YOU!
The man who kills man
The man who builds walls
The man who displaces
YOU!
The man who hates me
The man who hates you
Who controls our spaces
×2

vocal record scratches.
I wanna be free.
I wanna be free.
I wanna be free.
I wanna be free.

Rudi Goblen's
Fito. Photo: Maria
Baranova

song ends.

FITO *keeps the tambourine rattling at the tail end
of the song and throughout the silence.*

it leads him into the middle of the circle.

he sets it down.

THE FIRST TIME

monologue and movement inside the circle.

FITO
The first time
I witnessed an officer harassing someone
I was eleven years old.

He was Cuban.
A rookie officer.

[*beat*]

My *DARE*-to-keep-kids-off-drugs-teacher-in-
fifth-grade
picking on a Nicaraguan teenager—my
brother.

[*beat*]

We were playing basketball.
Officers then pulled up,
got out, stood by,
poked fun and laughed at us.
Officer then walked over,
threw a knife on the ground

and said, "Pick it up."

[*beat*]

Brother:

"Why? You threw it on the floor."

[*beat*]

Officer:
"So the second you grab it,
I can shoot you
and say it was in self-defense."

[*rest*]

Officer then bent down,
picked up the knife
looked my brother in his eyes on his way up
      and said,

[*beat*]

"Huh . . .

Pussy."

FITO *exits downstage of the circle.*

the musicians are left alone.

SAMSON

live music here. just musicians

song ends.

THE BEGINNING

FITO *enters the circle from stage right*

and moves throughout it while speaking.

Rudi Goblen's
Fito. Photo: Maria
Baranova

FITO
This all started
in Managua, Nicaragua,
on May 14, 1981,
at exactly 9:10 AM.

It was a Thursday.
I googled it.

Three years after my mother's family's fallout
and fumble into a dysfunctional home;
during a war there, we fled.
We came to the states and moved to
    California.

LA.

Eight years after being kicked out
and homeless,
two earthquakes,
a gang of gang violence,
our house getting shot up and broken into,
and me falling off a second-story roof onto a
    concrete sidewalk,
we fled again.
Moved to Miami.

Now, let's just fast-forward twenty-seven
    years
to the day of my naturalization ceremony into
    this country.
Find me there, standing, about to raise my
    hand.
I could see the light at the end of the tunnel.
But there were no angels playing trumpets,
or overwhelming sensation of warmth or
    peace.

As I looked closer, there was a girl.
There. Standing. Alone.

I couldn't see her as well as I could feel the
    way she looked.
And I couldn't hear her as well as I could
    smell the way she felt.
But I could never forget the sound of her
    smile, and knew it was her

the second she said

[*beat*]

"FITO."

[*beat*]

My mother.

[*beat*]

A wondrous woman for a wondrous moment.

And all of a sudden . . .

beatbox

[*HAH!*]

All of a sudden.
All I can think about was how DOPE AS FUCK
    MY MOM WAS YO.

Oh, which means:

in a white voice

My mother was an extraordinarily fine young
    lady if I say so myself.
And you without a doubt would absolutely
    concur if you would have ever
    encountered her presence.

[*beat*]

See Alicia's heart
[*pf, pf*] pumped
[*pf, pf*] pure
[*pf, pf*] profusely.

And . . .

beatbox

in one breath

You couldn't catch her hanging crooked if she
    was a frame dangling at an angle on a
    wall inside a home that was built on
    the side of a mountain that suddenly
    slightly fell off its foundation the exact
    same time the earth spun off its axis

while you were doing a handstand
trying to balance knowing you have no
equilibrium but you swear you sort of
saw her leaning like the Tower of Pisa.
Man please—uh.

You know she's honestly honest.

gasp

Honestly.
Straight up straight edge
from a rich family, she dropped out in the
sixth grade.
And when money and family went to shit,
still managed to open up a vegetarian
restaurant
where she taught yoga classes and baked the
bread herself.
Hookers, hippies, junkies,
and the gays were some of her best friends.
They took care of her; and her them in return.

She always said,
"Don't judge.
You never know whose help you might need
or who your kids can turn out to be in the
future.
Learn to love everyone."

And she did—*everyone*.

[*rest*]

The first time my mother saw a light at the
end of tunnel
was September 17, 1980. She was a few months
pregnant with me.
And she was on her way down to this
marketplace,
where she would go to sell some clothes and
shoes she would sew and design herself,
to make some extra money on the side 'cause
she had a second baby—me—on the
way.

But, on her way down there that afternoon,
as my mother went to cross the street,
my mother's life . . .

Spoke up.

lights shift.

FITO *quickly takes the tambourine from the floor.
on his knees, he begins to play like a toddler with
his toys.*

*his free hand is his mother walking and crossing
the street. the tambourine is the motorcycle that
will hit her.*

a slow-motion crash.

FITO *drops the tambourine out of his hand onto
the floor.*

he stands.

he sees his mother laying there.

Two broken wrists,
a shattered right knee
twenty-eight stitches on her head,
just to save me.

[*silence*]

My mother survived.

lights shift.

addressing the audience

And here she was, that day—today—
as I was about to raise my hand.
And all I could think about were the things I
never said,
the things I never did, and the things I've
never gave her.
All that cliché shit you hear people say.
But yo, it was true.
I wanted her to know that if I could, if I could,
I would celebrate her existence every day.
Every hour on the hour. 365 days a year.
A parade would fill the streets

blasting music she loved,
and we would crown her queen with a sash to
    match.
Feed her delicious fruits and desserts, and
        massage her until she was a big blob of
        stress-free.
Because she wanted it,
she needed it,
and she deserved it yo.

light shift.

And as I got closer
to lifting up my hand.
I wanted her to know,
at that very moment,
that she was,
is,
and always will be

[*beat*]

appreciated.

ALL WE CAN BE

live music here

FITO *improvises vocal percussion sounds to the
music before speaking.*

FITO
Listen as I talk
because tainted time is ticking in swirls.
And time after time,
we all pick scabs off this earth's back as ticks
    in this world.
Yet, fiction is living.
Pleasure and pain is giving.
And we all walk handstands on tightropes
with the earth and its hopes
on our mind over matter, soul over flesh
        blabber,
rather infatuated with the thought of
        thinking, which death is worst, sinking
        or splattered.

But fuck that.
I'm done uttering obscure.
And I've begun to make sure I soar shores
        through sores of metaphors.
Of course I coast the core cold and crack your
        cola while you croak on chrome,
so critic that country critters.
While still my will and wits litter a bit of the
        bitter tasting nation, that's lower casing
        placing,
the faces of our races, then claim capitals by
        statistics.
Bitch, I pump the pissed fist!
I'm pacifist with a pessimistic shit list.
'Cause this belongs to me.
I mean G.O.D. Actually, the all in we.
'Cause in reality,
you, me, and the planets make the all's energy
        and G.O.D. if not the WE if one speaks in
        fractions of exactly, see.
The future's fractured, b.
So extract me from your abstract scenery,
'cause surreal is so real to the all my soul can
        be,
which is just WE.
Not a slack-of-the-buck, back-of-the-truck,
        oh-shit-I'm-fucked-out-of-luck-crop-
        gathering paid-pennies-fruit picker.
Or that must-be-blind, comes-first-to-mind,
        for-a-country's-front-line, shield-of-
        fools-for-the-elite,
a first to catch the missile.
Sir, may the spic speak sir?!
You wanna harm me?
Shoot three of my limbs off for me to come
        back as a war hero nicknamed Army?
That's not all I can.
So to hell with your sorority glories,
and cloning our stories to make them false-
        fables.
The all in me which is the seed of energy
        knows they disable and label our truth.
So I give you nothing but the "oops,

95

Rudi Goblen's
Fito. Photo: Maria
Baranova

did I spit on your books for glorifying as
      heroes and not crooks?" song.
I'm on a vagabond die-with-your-boots-on-
      mission for the pawns to win the once-
      upon.
'Cause it's been a long, wrong song to me.
Son of man, a seed of energy, part of the G.O.D.
Actually, the all in we.
In reality.
You, me, and the planets make the all's energy
      and G.O.D. if not the WE
if one speaks in fractions of exactly.
So in these sands of insanity,
breathe along with your seeds
and soon we'll see that
we can
and shall be
all we can be
which is just
WE.

light shift

dance solo

FITO *is lured back into the circle.*

*before taking the final step to becoming a citizen,
he battles with the decision of what it means to be
sworn in to this country.*

*is he loyal to his family if he leaves a land that has
proven itself hateful and dangerous to his people?*

*does he embrace the danger/hate to gain a life his
ancestors could only have dreamed of?*

*taking specific images, movements, and gestures
from all of the stories and songs up to this point,
he dances a dance of struggle and freedom. restraints and relief. a cleansing.*

this dance ends with FITO *at the mic, buttoning
his suit, fixing his hair, and slowly raising his
hand. the musicians do the same behind him.*

96

THE OATH OF ALLEGIANCE

all three men look up to be sworn in.

FITO *slightly mouths the words as he repeats what is being said to them.*

VOICE-OVER/FITO
I hereby declare,
on oath,
that I absolutely
and entirely
renounce and abjure
all allegiance and fidelity
to any foreign prince,
potentate,
state,
or sovereignty
of whom or which
I have heretofore been a subject or citizen;
that I will support
and defend
the Constitution and laws
of the United States of America
against all enemies,
foreign and domestic;
that I will bear true faith
and allegiance
to the same;

voice-over gradually distorts
it is frightening

that I will bear arms
on behalf of the United States
when required by the law;
that I will perform noncombatant service
in the Armed Forces of the United States
when required by the law;
that I will perform work
of national importance under civilian direction
when required by the law;
and that I take this obligation freely
without any mental reservation
or purpose

of evasion;
so help me God.

[*beat*]

FITO
Help me God.

[*beat*]

Help me.

[*beat*]

Help.

[*beat*]

ANDROID (*voice-over*)
Welcome.

blackout

SHAKEM

lights bump on for cast acknowledgments,

goodbyes, and thank yous.

musicians perform.

audience is invited to dance in the circle.

END OF PLAY

Keep up to date on new scholarship

Issue alerts are a great way to stay current on all the cutting-edge scholarship from your favorite Duke University Press journals. This free service delivers tables of contents directly to your inbox, informing you of the latest groundbreaking work as soon as it is published.

To sign up for issue alerts:

1. Visit **dukeu.press/register** and register for an account. You do not need to provide a customer number.

2. After registering, visit **dukeu.press/alerts**.

3. Go to "Latest Issue Alerts" and click on "Add Alerts."

4. Select as many publications as you would like from the pop-up window and click "Add Alerts."

read.dukeupress.edu/journals